Contents

©CLPE 2002

ISBN 1 872267 26 2

Published by
Centre for Literacy in Primary Education
Webber Street
London SE1 8QW
Registered Charity No. 1092698

Tel: 0207 401 3382
     0207 633 0840
Fax: 0207 928 4624

e-mail: info@clpe.co.uk
www.clpe.co.uk

Editors:
Myra Barrs
Sue Pidgeon

Photography:
Phil Polglaze

Printed by DS Print/Redesign

Produced by Maddison Graphics

Acknowledgements

We thank Brenda Hockley and Iris Scott (CLPE) for their work on the manuscript and Ann Lazim (CLPE) for her work on the references.

We thank all schools who have given us permission to use photographs of their classrooms.

We thank the pupils in the schools for the examples of their work.

We thank all the teachers involved in the Boys and Writing Project for their contributions.

Elizabeth Baker, Woodacre Special School, Thurrock

Christine Barnes, Sir Francis Drake Primary School, Lewisham

Linda Benton, Davidson Junior School, Croydon

Sue Bown, Stifford Primary School, Thurrock

Patricia Chaudhry, Quarry Hill Infant School, Thurrock

Jenni Clarke, St. Saviours Primary School, Waltham Fores

Samantha Fenn, Highwood Primary School, Hertfordshire

Rachel Green, Woodside Infant School, Waltham Forest

Sue Hirschheimer, Tunstall Nursery School, Croydon

Sue McGonigle, Lee Manor Primary School, Lewisham

Mary Jo McPherson, Torridon Junior School, Lewisham

Louisa Marock, Chater Junior School, Hertfordshire

Heidi Morgan, Wittingham Primary School, Waltham Forest

Alan North, Fairlop Primary School, Redbridge

Victoria Purbrick, Abbots Hall Junior School, Thurrock

Emma Scott-Stevens, Chafford Hundred Campus, Thurrock

Michelle Shanahan, Highwood Primary School, Hertfordshire

Evalina Strum, Wellington Primary School, Waltham Forest

Jenny Vernon, Isaac Newton PDC, Kensington & Chelsea

Laura Ward, Cleveland Junior School, Redbridge

We thank Penguin Books for permission to reproduce two pages from the Dorling Kindersley *Eyewitness Guide: Ancient Rome*.

Boys' underachievement in writing is well documented as an issue for primary schools; the CLPE Boys and Writing project gave teachers the opportunity to develop strategies in their classrooms to raise writing standards and to share their practice more widely with other teachers.

CHAPTER 1

Boys and Writing:
Introduction

Sue Pidgeon

Background

This book is the fourth in a series of CLPE publications about gender and literacy that reflect growing interest in the subject, work with teachers and also the way the agenda on gender and literacy has changed. Back in 1986, our first tentative foray into the debate was a Language and Gender edition of *Language Matters*. Here the focus was mainly on how teachers tried to redress the sex stereotyping in books and in the media through their choice of reading materials and topics for writing. Looking at this issue now, it is curiously outdated in tone, harking back to a time when we were focusing on changing 'the world out there' rather than pedagogy in classrooms. Trying to bring 'the world out there' into the classrooms was the theme of the first course we ran on gender and literacy at CLPE – but that foundered as several of the participants left the room in protest when we began to discuss the use of children's TV (and superheroes in particular) as a valid text type for boys.

By the time *Reading the Difference* was published in 1993 the agenda was changing. There was more interest in the differences between boys and girls as readers, and the beginnings of interest in why boys were not achieving as well as girls in literacy (it is easy to forget that the equalities agenda for the previous twenty years had really focused on girls' achievement). We continued the practice of identifying and working with teachers who were pushing back the boundaries in their own practice and this note still comes through in the book. Teachers writing in this book were listening to children to get insights into their perceptions and preferences, debating these with boys and girls in their classrooms, and extending practice to provide a range of literacy

...the debate around gender and literacy had turned to one around boys' underachievement in literacy and it had also become a much more public debate.

experiences that met the needs of all the children in their class.

By 1998, when *Boys and Reading* was published, the debate around gender and literacy had turned to one around boys' underachievement in literacy and it had also become a much more public debate. Courses and conferences on the subject were well attended and teachers were actively searching and researching their classroom practice for examples of strategies to support boys to achieve (but not at the expense of girls). Four years on the debate about gender patterns in literacy learning continues, and generates interest way beyond the sphere of education. But the issues around boys' underachievement remain, and this underachievement is most marked in literacy, particularly in writing.

The accessibility of attainment data is one factor that has helped to focus the agenda on the differences between boys' and girls' attainment. All the details are now easily accessed from the DFESwebsite (www.standards.dfes.gov.uk/ genderandachievment).

Girls do better now in all subjects but the difference is most pronounced in literacy. As standards in literacy in primary schools have risen, the gap between boys' and girls' achievement has remained remarkably constant. Over the last four years (1998-2002) attainment in the KS2 English test has risen from 71% to 75% but the gap between the number of boys and girls reaching this level remains at about 10%. Inclusion and 'narrowing the differentials' are current national priorities and continue to lead the focus on boys' underachievement. LEAs are now able to make more sophisticated analysis of their attainment data against free school meals, ethnicity and children with English as an Additional Language, but these differences do not affect the marked underachievement of boys in literacy.

However it is when the data is broken down into reading and writing that we see the biggest gap between boys' and girls' attainment. At Key Stage 2 in 2002 77% boys and 83% girls achieved level 4 and above in reading and 52% boys and 67% girls achieved level 4 and above in writing. The difference in boys' and girls' attainment is 6% in reading and 15% in writing. A focus on boys and writing is therefore absolutely pertinent at this time.

Data at national and local level show the same differentials in performance. But at school level the situation is very different. It has always been clear that the aggregated data masks a multitude of practices – and that although boys in general are doing less well in literacy, there are many schools where they are achieving as well as girls (and others where the gap between girls' and boys' attainment is far greater than the national one).

Examining effective practice has been the focus of our work with teachers – both to investigate what makes for effective practice, and to share this analysis with other practitioners. *Boys and Reading* (1998) was the product of the work of a focus group of interested teachers who documented what they were doing in their classrooms as examples of good practice. It was logical to follow this by looking at boys and writing and in Summer 2000 we set up the CLPE Boys and Writing project.

The aim of the project was to work with experienced teachers over a period of time to build up a picture of how best to support boys with writing. The project was planned to:

...it is when the data is broken down into reading and writing that we see the biggest gap between boys' and girls' attainment.

- Consider the issues around boys and writing
- Identify effective teaching strategies
- Use this analysis to plan and carry out some specific teaching
- Evaluate the impact of this work and develop effective models of teaching writing with boys in mind
- Share evidence of effective practice within LEAs and across participating LEAS

The aim of this book is not only to present the work from the project but also to move forward the discussion and debate around boys and writing. This introduction gives an overview of the Boys and Writing project, how it was structured and the main findings from the participating teachers. The book includes small-scale case studies from teachers on the project and also branches out to include contributions from researchers and educationalists working in this field.

The Project Design and programme

The Boys and Writing project ran from Summer 2000 to Spring 2001. It included four days of central training, four days' release to work in school, one day for writing up the project and a final presentation conference in March to share outcomes and best practice. LEAs were invited to participate, using the Standards Fund, and the twenty teachers involved came from seven LEAs. They were all experienced teachers and included headteachers, deputies and a consultant. They were working in a range of settings: from Nursery to KS3, mainstream and special education. Some teachers had already been involved in work on boys and literacy, for others this was the first time they had specifically focused on it. They shared an interest in the subject and the quality of their contributions throughout and the informal discussion and sharing of practice was a significant feature of the project.

From the start the taught sessions combined opportunities to share and discuss current practice with input from the tutors and outside speakers. Over the project the sessions covered differences in attainment, observed differences in writing content and style, teaching strategies, use of drama and role play, using ICT, and target setting. The participants had the opportunity to hear from Lynda Graham about the Croydon Writing project. This project exemplifies the benefits of classroom research and Lynda Graham's account of it is included in this book under the title: 'Teachers as Experts in Learning'. From CLPE Myra Barrs talked about the CLPE Reader and the Writer project and Olivia O'Sullivan provided a workshop about the links between Literacy and ICT.

These taught sessions provided the starting points for discussion and reflection. There is no large body of research evidence on boys and writing and so on the course we were trying to draw together strands that might be related, and reinterpret what we knew about children's writing. Some initial discussion focused on perceived differences between boys and girls in relation to transcriptional elements in writing – spelling and handwriting – but the participants' main interest was in the writing process. The course evaluation forms reflected participants' growing awareness of the issues. One wrote: 'I was particularly interested in links with writing and thinking and that children need time to think and develop their thoughts'. Another noted: 'The notion that children need time to 'play' with their writing and have ownership of it has come across very strongly'.

Planning and organising the in-school project was the other theme for the INSET days and participants began to design their in-school project on the first day. Because the focus was on raising attainment the teachers were asked to identify a group of children to work with and to assess this group in terms of both their attainment and their motivation, so that they would be able to evaluate the impact of the work. As a follow-up from each taught session the teachers identified some aspect or some activity to try out. Time was built into each session for 'discussion partners' to feed back on what they were trying out and to share with each other, as 'critical friends', their ideas and designs for their projects. Some teachers had a clear idea of an area to follow up; others tried out a number before deciding on a specific area of focus for their project. This shared planning allayed some of the anxiety about the project, although the anxiety about the final presentation continued! Discussions with tutors and colleagues helped to clarify ideas arising from the work in school, so that work was soon well under way and ready for the

As the project developed certain themes around boys' writing were emerging.

HMI say: 'Boys' participation improves significantly when the work requires an active response'.

presentation conference in March.

Emerging themes

As the project developed certain themes around boys' writing were emerging. These themes were an important part of the development of the project as they helped to group together a number of different areas of investigation in a more coherent structure. Boys and Writing is a very large and complex area to investigate; success in this area depends on good practice in teaching writing, but to teach boys effectively practice must go deeper or further. What we are constantly trying to do is to isolate a number of practices or activities that may make a difference– but we also need to acknowledge that it will probably be a combination of a number of factors that makes the difference. In order to explore this question it was important to return to the complexities of the writing process and engage again with the debate around the effective teaching of writing. Myra Barrs' chapter comprehensively lays out the theoretical framework to the teaching of writing and raises the issues that we needed to take into account.

A focus on effective teaching was a strand running through the project. Many of the strategies previously promoted as supporting boys' learning, such as scaffolding, learning through shared reading and writing, and the use of paired work, are now far more firmly established in classrooms as part of the National Literacy Strategy and so have been influential in raising standards. Course participants saw these as a normal part of their teaching. However there still remain great differences between pedagogical practices in literacy teaching in classrooms across the country. The HMI evaluation of the third year of the NLS again points out the differences between the attainment of boys and girls and particularly notes differences in response in literacy lessons. Although HMI see many improvements in literacy teaching, they observe that the response of girls in literacy lessons is significantly better than that of boys. They say: 'Boys' participation improves significantly when the work requires an active response'. The examples they give of this: good choices of subject matter, the use of speaking and listening, making links to first hand experience, are all ones that were picked up on the Boys and Writing project.

In the project, two key themes began to emerge, one around attitudes to writing and the other around the use of oral and visual support for writing. These are in many ways two aspects of the same coin. One is about finding ways to address and support some boys' antipathy to writing; the other is about finding 'ways into writing' that will support boys' identified interests and preferences.

Unwilling to write – developing confidence and motivation

Once the teachers on the project had identified a group of 'underachieving boys' to work with, a common strand running through discussions about these boys was the boys general lack of interest in writing, compounded further by their unwillingness to return to, review or revise their work.

Some project teachers had identified strategies to use when working with these children to help them to feel more positive about the writing process. Both Christine Barnes and Laura Ward looked at ways to help boys with revising and editing their work, while Alan North studied the use of targets and explicit discussion of writing. Christine Barnes focused particularly on conferencing with two boys in her Year 5 class. She found that they both were able confidently to articulate preferences in reading and writing but were less confident in reflecting individually on their own writing and their progress. Christine helped them work together to revise a story; they identified key features to improve their story and evaluated their writing against these. Alun North similarly found that opportunities for explicit discussion with a group of boys about their writing helped them to be clear about their progress and the next steps they needed to take. Setting writing targets with them helped them to clarify where they were going. Laura Ward made explicit to her class the process of revising work. She found that this, along with focusing on the audience for the work, provided useful support for writing. She stressed the importance of working with a talk or revision partner as a very useful strategy. She also provided very clear support for revision checklists and guides for writing partners) but noted that establishing these practices was likely to be a long process.

Although the teachers mentioned above

focused on making explicit the process of revision they all included opportunities to clarify with their group the purposes for writing, particularly to support motivation in writing. Several teachers had noted that their targeted group seemed to prefer activities where they had some choice or where a challenge was set. Linda Benton and Victoria Purbrick both took this further by giving children more choice over the content of writing, to see if this supported motivation. They took from Lynda Graham's work with teachers in Croydon the idea of writing journals. Linda Benton noted that the children responded 'almost with disbelief' to the opportunity to write about anything, and most set about it with enthusiasm, but that children's having control over content was not by itself enough to improve the quality of the writing. Victoria Purbrick's account of her homework writing journal is included in chapter 6. This issue of choice and challenge was also taken on by Louisa Marock who set a weekly story challenge for a pair of pupils and noted that when working together they achieved more than they usually did alone. In Elizabeth Baker and Emma Scott Stevens' chapters you can read about how they examined the attitudes and experiences of boys with writing in a special and a secondary school respectively.

An unexpected outcome of this work was the benefit that the targeted group gained from having the opportunity to work with the teacher. Christine Barnes noted that the boys 'were pleased to be chosen'. Evalina Strums' comments about the 'unwilling to write' group she was working with were particularly striking. She noted that, to her surprise, although the group of Year 6 boys she was studying presented themselves as confident and were major contributors to discussions, they lacked confidence in their writing and wanted considerable reassurance from her that they were doing the right thing. The boys gained in confidence through this work. Confidence is a crucial aspect of effective writing – having the confidence to take risks and to try things out, being prepared not to get everything right. This is an aspect of teaching and learning that we need to take more seriously, particularly for this group of boys.

> An unexpected outcome of this work was the benefit that the targeted group gained from having the opportunity to work with the teacher.

Ways into writing – spoken & visual

The other key theme that emerged was the benefits that came from providing some boys with ways into writing – ways that they felt familiar with and where they could succeed. Visual stimuli, ICT and video were ways that were quickly identified. Drama, play and storytelling were found to be equally powerful.

Several teachers were inspired to follow up Myra Barrs' description of the use of drama and storytelling in the Reader and the Writer project. The importance of oral rehearsal, of talk for writing, links all the themes in this book. Sometimes this is talk that helps boys to discuss and articulate their writing or to shape and refine their ideas; sometimes it is talk which enables pupils to get into the fictional situation and the characters more fully. Included in this book Mary Jo McPhersons's account of the use of storytelling to develop a sense of audience, Sue Bown's account of drama and video to stimulate writing and Sue Hirschheimer's report of how writing and play are linked in her Nursery School. Each of these teachers saw the impact of oral experiences in the writing, as could Heidi Morgan who linked drama to writing in her history project on the Tudors. This remains a relatively new area, but all the feedback from teachers who have used drama to support writing, indicate that it is very influential in improving the quality of writing, particularly for the 'can and don't' boys.

Clear differences between boys' and girls' interest and expertise in ICT emerged. Samantha Fenn found that giving a group of low-achieving boys in Year 2 the opportunity to use 'Clicker' in their writing was remarkably effective. Sue McGonigle's account of using the World Wide Web and the 'Hyper-studio' programme with a group of boys is included here. Louisa Marock introduced another dimension when she noted that the best writing the boys in her class had done was in response to the Toy Story video. Jenni Clarke used a number of visual prompts as stimuli for writing with her group – but this was a relatively unexplored area, although course members generally agreed that they could see the influence of visual media in the content and sometimes the structure of boys' writing. In this book, additional chapters from well-known writers in this field take this question further. Gemma Moss explores the increasingly visual nature of non-fiction texts and explores how these influences structure of non-fiction writing. Eve Bearne moves the discussion of subject matter in children's writing beyond stereotyping to a more sophisticated analysis of the visual sources that children draw on in their writing

The project outcomes

The Project teachers' evaluations of progress made it clear that all boys had benefited from the additional support in terms of confidence, that some had benefited in terms of motivation and that the writing produced as a result of the various inputs was of a higher standard than previously. It is obviously impossible to isolate the variables and attribute improvements to any one strategy or experience. However, it seems clear that there are a number of strategies that can

> The importance of oral rehearsal, of talk for writing, links all the themes in this book.

contribute to boys improving their writing and that they hinge on improving motivation, attitude and purpose and the use of oral and visual support. Through everything runs the river of talk for writing and talk about writing. This reflects the fundamental point that came up again and again in the project – good practice in teaching writing benefits all pupils.

The accounts of the course members' projects that we have included here give insights into what they did in their classes and their schools and what they achieved. This sharing of good practice is a powerful agent for change and we would hope that here are experiences, ideas and suggestions that will resonate with other teachers. Each teacher's work on the project contributes to the wider research picture of Boys and Writing

Finally the end-of-course Boys and Writing Conference was a fitting marker to the end of the project and to the work of the participants. The teachers presented their work to an audience of colleagues, headteachers, advisers and consultants, and the conference helped to pull out the underlying themes and common strands.

Beyond the project

In the year since the project ended, 'boys and writing' has continued to be a topic of widespread interest. Training, workshops and conferences on this topic have been well attended. Across the country in schools, colleges and LEAs, teachers and educators are developing training and support around the issues of boys' underachievement. Also there is a national DfES project looking at Raising Boys' Achievement. This book is a contribution to the national debate.

In 2003 a new research project on boys and literacy will begin at CLPE. We expect that this new research will build on some of the insights that have emerged from the Boys and Writing project, and we hope that it will take thinking on this challenging topic still further.

Sue Pidgeon

References

Barrs, Myra and Pidgeon, Sue (1986) 'Gender and Reading' *Language Matters* 1986 No 1
Barrs, Myra and Pidgeon, Sue, eds. (1993) *Reading the Difference* London, CLPE
Barrs, Myra and Pidgeon, Sue, eds. (1998) *Boys and Reading* London, CLPE
Barrs, Myra and Cork, Valerie (2001) *The Reader in the Writer* London, CLPE
HMI (2001)*The National Literacy Strategy: the third year. An evaluation by HMI* London, Ofsted

CHAPTER 2

Tools for change

Myra Barrs

Reading and writing can help to change the way we see ourselves and see the world. But boys are often less experienced readers, and this can affect their development in writing. As governments worry about the gap between girls' and boys' achievement in literacy, we need to be aware that in some classrooms the gap is being narrowed.

Reading and writing are ways of talking, thinking, living and working on paper. They are what Vygotsky called 'psychological tools', which is to say that they help us to act on the world - not in a physical way, but through the symbol system of written language. We learn to use them to represent the world and our stories and ideas about it, and to share in others' ideas and stories. Writing comes before reading of course, but reading is usually what we think it is most important to teach young children.

Psychological tools, according to Vygotsky, have a particular property, in that they are reversible. They act not only outwards but inwards, they turn back on their users, shape them and change them. Vygotsky thought that it was through the use of these kinds of psychological tools that human beings developed themselves mentally. Learning to read and write viewed in this way become not just important means of taking part in what David Olson calls 'The World on Paper' – the enormous mental universe that reading and writing admit us to. They are also ways of changing the way we think, extending the way we are, becoming more. And our sense of ourselves as gendered beings is one of the things that reading and writing may extend and change.

Reading histories

The reading history of a person reveals this process at work. All of us are walking anthologies of the texts we have read, texts which have in some sense stayed with us. Books and other texts affect children's views of themselves, including their views of gender identity. We all take our view of gender identity and how it is marked partly from what we find in texts, including media texts – many of which are strongly stereotyped.

> **Part of growing up is the discovery of more complex ways of being, including being female/male**

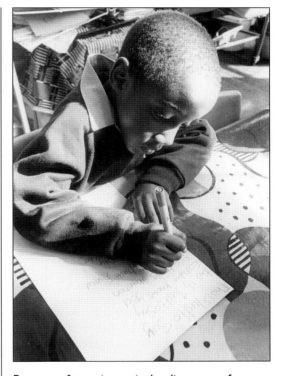

But part of growing up is the discovery of more complex ways of being, including being female/male. Reading helps in these discoveries; in certain circumstances it can be a major route to discovery. Growing up in a Midlands suburb in the 1950s, I found that the books I read offered me far more varied ways of being female than the world around me ever did.

Initially of course, we may opt for the stereotypes and indeed desire them. A girl reader whom I know well (my god-daughter) was, as a pre-school child, obsessed with all things frilly and feminine. Her reading history shows a progression from this kind of obsession with marking gender in early childhood, towards an appreciation of a wider range of possible ways of being.

* She recalls that as a little girl her favourite book was *The Twelve Dancing Princesses*, the story of twelve princesses who secretly go dancing night after night. Each night they put on a different dress and a new pair of shoes – which they wear out by dancing through the night. The story is about a world which is one long dancing party; the day is for nothing but sleeping. The excitement of the situation mainly comes from dressing up and getting ready for the party, and from escaping the attention of the adults who would stop you from going. This was Laurie's shoe-fetishist period, and I am sure that the endless pairs of new shoes that feature in the story were part of what fascinated her most about this book.

• When she was eleven or twelve, she read through the complete works of Joan Aiken. She especially liked *Night Birds on Nantucket* (Aiken 1966), in which the heroine is the resourceful and funny Dido Twite, a splendidly outspoken, strong-minded and fearless character. Laurie's father is American. She said about this book: "My Dad, when he was a little boy, he used to go to Nantucket for his holiday and because Nantucket is such a tiny island he had known all the places and he would say, I've been there." She added, "I find I like books where I can believe slightly they have something to do with me."

• At fifteen her favourite reading were the collected works of Sara Paretsky, with her detective novels about V.I. Warshawski, a female private eye in Los Angeles. The improbable heroics of Paretsky's main character engaged her for a period. During this time she was wondering whether she might like to be a policewoman: she is very tall and height seemed to be an asset in that world. She soon abandoned this idea, as she did the books, once she had read them all.

The progress between these texts clearly has a lot to do with Laurie revising her ideas about possible ways of being active and powerful in the world. All of her reading choices seem to exemplify ways of going beyond the constraints of childhood and adolescence into the unknown, daunting and desirable world of adulthood. All speak about her personally in some fundamental way. Some of the progression between these texts transparently concerns ideas of femaleness and suggests that she is changing her views of how girls and women can be in the world.

I can parallel this history with other reading histories of girls but I don't know whether many boys' histories would show the same kind of pattern, of a view of gender becoming more complex, problematic, and varied. Do boys have anything like the same possibility of broadening their ideas of what it is to be male through their reading? Is there a way in which

girls, in the contemporary world, have access to a wider range of possible ways of being? Girls, as we pointed out in *Boys and Reading*, are far readier to read books about boys than boys are to read books about girls, and girls are far freer to act out male roles than boys are to act out female roles.

Heroic legends

Zora Neale Hurston, one of the twentieth century's greatest black writers, describes in her autobiography *Dust Tracks on a Road* (1986) an important event in her own reading history. She was a pupil in a village schoolroom in Orange County Florida when two white women came to visit. This kind of visit was not uncommon:

"The whites who came down from the North were often brought by their friends to visit the village school. A Negro school was something strange to them and while they were always sympathetic and kind, curiosity must have been present also."

Hurston recalls being called up to read to the visitors. She had already devoured the lesson that was being read, the story of Pluto and Persephone, and she gave the reading all she'd got:

"This Graeco-Roman myth was one of my favourites. I was exalted by it and that is the way I read my paragraph:

'Yes, Jupiter had seen her (Persephone). He had seen the maiden picking flowers in the field. He had seen the chariot of the dark monarch pause by the maiden's side. He had seen him when he seized Persephone. He had seen the black horses leap down Mt Aetna's fiery throat. Persephone was now in Pluto's dark realm and he had made her his wife.'

The two women looked at each other and then back to me. Mr Calhoun broke out in a proud smile beneath his bristling moustache and instead of the next child taking up where I had ended he nodded to me to go on".

Hurston was allowed to read the whole story through and next day was invited to go to the Northerners' hotel for another display of her reading. When the women went back up North they sent her a huge box of clothing and, better still, books:

"In that box were Gulliver's Travels, Grimms' Fairy Tales, Dick Whittington, Greek and Roman myths and, best of all, Norse Tales. Why did the Norse Tales strike so deeply into my soul? I do not know, but they did. I seemed to remember seeing Thor swing his mighty short-handled hammer as he sped across the sky in rumbling thunder, lightning flashing from the tread of his steeds and the wheels of his chariot....Of the Greeks, Hercules moved me

> Some of the progression between these texts transparently concerns ideas of femaleness and suggests that she is changing her views of how girls and women can be in the world.

most. I followed him eagerly on his tasks. The story of the choice of Hercules as a boy when he met Pleasure and Duty and put his hand in that of Duty and followed her steep way to the blue hills of fame and glory, which she pointed out at the end, moved me profoundly. I resolved to be like him....".

Zora Neale Hurston was an intelligent, pugnacious, spirited and outstandingly gifted woman who never accepted any limits on her right to make herself as she pleased. As a much younger girl she had once proposed to a friend that they should set off to find the end of the world (the friend never turned up). The books she vibrated to so strongly, especially the heroic legends with their tales of strength, struggle and endurance, seemed to be speaking to her directly. They must have expressed some underlying desire of hers to build her courage in order to confront a wider world than the one she knew. All are exaggeratedly male legends in which the heroes, like her, are – in her words – "keen to attack the world, bite it off and chew it". Hurston took from these heroic fantasies the aspects that she needed, already knowing that she must go beyond the context that she had been born into and that she would one day indeed set off to find the end of that world. Through her reading she was learning that it was possible to change her life. As a black woman from the South, she needed that conviction.

But she was also learning about writing. In time she became a writer herself, and one who made the novel change and treat experiences that had been left out of American literature. As she wrote she drew on the resources of her reading, and also on the oral language resources of the African-American people that she mainly wrote about. Her reading had been part of her route into learning to write. Many writers have testified to the importance of the way in which their own writing is rooted in their reading. Susan Price, the children's writer whose retellings of folk tales have created new exciting novels for children, says about her own growth as a writer "I've learned more from folk story and folk ballad than I've ever learned from any other kind of language....I learnt it not by thought or by study but by constant reading and listening to folk story".

Learning about writing through reading

Perhaps it is a truism that we learn a lot about writing from our reading, but in any consideration of gender and literacy it is important to give full weight to this thing that we all know in our bones. The National Literacy Strategy has put a new emphasis on the direct teaching of writing, but we should be aware that the most basic way of learning written language is still likely to be reading. Through reading

We should be aware that the most basic way of learning written language is still likely to be reading

children experience many kinds of written texts, becoming attuned to their linguistic structures and rhythms, their generic markers, language registers, forms and conventions.

A recent piece of research by CLPE (*The Reader in the Writer*, 2001) was designed to find out what kind of influence children's reading of literature had on their writing development. The findings showed that this influence was widespread. Children who had studied challenging literary texts, and heard them read aloud, were able to take on the tunes and rhythms of these texts, to echo their patterns of language, adopt their characteristic structures, and compose in their style, sometimes simply by recalling the language of the original, but also by creating their own episodes in the style of the original. They drew constantly on their ability to shadow, imitate and echo the original texts. Boys as well as girls used these ways of learning from texts, and as they did so their writing moved on visibly.

It is important to note that in our research children were not being asked to write in the style of the original mainly as a linguistic exercise, nor were they being given direct instruction in styles of writing. The theory behind the research was that the reading of literature in itself is likely to exercise an influence on writing and so we wanted to see what children took from the texts that they were meeting. It was evident that one of the most basic forms of learning they were using was imitation - but this was not just copying or imitation of any routine or formalistic kind. Whereas in the NLS publication *Grammar for Writing*, the focus is on analysing the grammatical features of texts and learning to use these features, in our research the focus was on the literary text itself, both for its meaning and also for its style or voice.

Learning to write under the influence of a powerful text such as Henrietta Branford's *Fire Bed and Bone* is principally about entering imaginatively into the world of the text and only secondarily looking at its linguistic patterns. When Sophie, one of our case study children, writes "I heard the wolves again last night howling at the tops of their voice, long and loud, big and bold. I lay with shivers all over my body", it is clear that she has taken on Henrietta Branford's style and is using it independently. None of this text appears in the original. Sophie has begun to write in the same voice as Branford's narrator: she is using imaginative imitation, but her focus is on the imagined experience rather than on the words.

Boys who avoid writing

If boys in general read less than girls (and we know they do) then they are simply getting less experience of written language, and fewer of what Margaret Meek Spencer calls the 'untaught lessons' that texts teach – about writing as well as reading. In a recent piece of research based at Southampton University, Gemma Moss (1998) found strong patterns of gender differentiation in the classes of seven to nine year olds that she studied. The research team divided the children they observed into three categories: children who can and do read freely in a self motivated way ("can/do"); children who can read but who don't read voluntarily ("can/don't"); children who can't yet read independently and who don't choose to read ("can't/don't"). (They based the can/can't distinction on teachers' assessments of children's competence and independence). The project data showed that there were more boys than girls in both the "can/don't" and the "can't/don't" categories.

Moss and her team found that "can't/don't" boys were anxious to mask their failure as

readers. They put a lot of energy into avoiding reading, especially in classrooms where teachers' judgements of reading proficiency were made highly visible (e.g. by the use of ability groupings, or by the kind of graded books provided for weaker readers). In these circumstances these boys would "do almost anything not to read". Girls in the "can't/don't" category, however, reacted differently to proficiency judgements, accepted the materials

> If boys in general read less than girls (and we know they do) then they are simply getting less experience of written language

they were assigned by the teacher and were prepared to spend more time reading.

Boys who were weaker readers often chose nonfiction in preference to fiction, but Moss concluded that this was mainly because nonfiction texts were not as obviously "graded" as nearly all the available fiction was:

"Nonfiction texts allow weaker boy readers to escape others' judgements about how well they read and how competent they are. They enable them to maintain self-esteem in the competitive environment of their peer-group relationships" (Moss, 1998).

In contrast, Moss found more girls than boys in the can/do category. Quantitative data showed that girls networked more around texts: they were more likely to use friends' recommendations to guide their reading and to share their reading with others.

Moss suggests that current theories about boys as readers may well be flawed:

"The commonsense view of why boys do less well at reading starts from the assumption that either boys' preferences in reading material are insufficiently represented in the classroom, or that boys see too few men reading to aspire to become readers themselves. Neither position is borne out by the Project data." (Moss, 1998.)

Peer group relationships

Instead, she highlights the different ways in which girls and boys react to proficiency judgements about their reading and the power of the peer group. Boys' peer group relationships tend to work against their choosing to read; the "status politics of boys' peer group culture" make it hard for them to be seen engaging in official literacy activities.

Girls' peer group relationships on the other hand seem on the whole to support their involvement in literacy. Whereas boys in Moss's "can/do" category nearly always came from homes where at least one parent was a committed reader, this was not true of girls, who seemed able to become committed readers via their peers and via the school. Groups of girls spend much more time in reading and networking around books.

In writing, other studies have found girls writing more, choosing to write more readily, and being more 'self-starting' as writers; that is they need less support to actually get launched on a piece of writing (Millard 1997). This is a major asset in a writer. To have the confidence to begin writing, to be able to get past the initial barrier of feeling daunted by a blank page, is one of the basic things a writer needs. To some extent this facility comes with practice, but it is also born out of a sense of enjoying writing as an activity. Confidence grows as experience increases:

writers who write regularly find more ways of tapping into their material and getting started. More girls than boys are likely to have this kind of confirming experience, because they are simply engaging more often with writing.

Millard also reports that, in writing, more boys are likely to get stuck before they start and to report themselves as having "difficulty in getting ideas". They would often like to make more use of pictures and graphics in planning their writing, as they do when they write at home. Many commentators have observed that many boys by preference intersperse writing and drawing, or prepare for writing by drawing the story they then go on to tell in words (Barrs 1988).

Moreover, boys are more likely to perceive technical accuracy, spelling and handwriting as the most important aspects of writing, and to feel daunted by writing because of the possibilities of error (Millard 1997). The Croydon Writing Project, which Lynda Graham writes about in this book, found boys saying things like "The most important things about writing are spelling and handwriting". Although teachers may not mean to give these messages to children, it seems that many children, especially boys, perceive technical accuracy as the key factor in writing, and see themselves as being bad at writing because of this. A recent study of 400 Ohio school students in grades four, six and eight, by Shelley Peterson, a professor at the University of Toronto showed that young males viewed themselves as less competent writers than their female counterparts:

"The students were asked to determine the gender of the authors of nine stories written by other Ohio students in a neighbouring district. The study found that the students perceived the author to be female if the stories were descriptive and well written, and male if the stories had spelling errors and poor grammar." (Peterson, 2001).

A Quebec government report points to the circular way in which the perception of girls' greater competence in literacy helps to produce the kinds of resistance and avoidance behaviour in boys that Gemma Moss noted in the classrooms she studied:

"Girls' greater proficiency in reading and writing is a reality perceived by both students and teachers. Therefore, both tend to see reading and writing as 'feminine'. This perception influences teachers' behaviour in the classroom. At the same time boys, under peer pressure, try to avoid being associated with these 'feminine' areas of learning."
Conseil Superieur de l'education

The report, by the Conseil Superieur de l'Education in Quebec, provides a thorough and reasoned account of a phenomenon which is

> It's important to acknowledge that there are large societal factors at work in this, and that there are limits to what schools are likely to achieve on their own

not confined to the UK but is widespread. Girls outperformed boys in all nine developed countries included in a recent literacy survey. (NFER). The Quebec report also makes important points about the social differences that complicate issues of gender and literacy ("While the gap between boys' and girls' academic achievement is evident in all social strata, the humbler the origins, the wider the gap will be"). It suggests that "working class boys who are experiencing academic difficulties are also those who most strongly support masculine stereotypes …in their case the negative impact of social class and gender is compounded" (because they are more likely to resist or avoid the official school agenda). It's important to acknowledge that there are large societal factors at work in this, and that there are limits to what schools are likely to achieve on their own. The Quebec paper concludes with a set of suggested policy guidelines and recommendations for short-term, medium-term and long-term measures; a set of proposals for concrete action at national level and also at the level of schools and research and training institutions.

Measurement-based thinking

But while we need to welcome the growing realisation at governmental level that there is an issue to be addressed here, there is also a danger that the current official focus on boys' underachievement in literacy is helping to *reinforce* the perceptions of teachers and support the general view of literacy as a 'feminine' area. It is certainly leading to a tendency to lump all boys together, instead of seeing the considerable differences between them. All measurement-based thinking tends to do this, as David Boyle points out in his useful book, *The Tyranny of Numbers: Why Counting Won't Make Us Happy* (2001). Boyle lists a number of what he terms 'counting paradoxes' to be found in a measurement culture. His list begins, "Counting Paradox 1: You can count people but you can't count individuals". By lumping people together you lose any sense of their individuality and difference. When test scores are aggregated the overall sums obscure what can be extreme differences within a class, within a school, or indeed within an LEA. To understand the world and make a difference to it we need to attend to reality, not to statistical abstractions, to real individual cases and their peculiarities, not to notional averages. This is where teachers have to start.

One of the sharp concerns that both government and schools now have about boys in the UK is that they may pull down national assessment scores. In a high stakes climate, it suddenly becomes urgent to boost boys' attainment, and there have been many national and local initiatives to attempt to achieve this.

Teaching to the test is becoming routine in the English educational system. Michael Fullan and his colleagues at the University of Toronto warned, in their second evaluation of the National Literacy and Numeracy Strategies, that:

"Of most concern are two practices – diverting time from teaching the curriculum to teaching pupils how to take the tests, especially in the months directly before the tests are given, and shifting time away from non-tested subjects to tested subjects".

The evaluation team also pointed out that:

"A preoccupation with single achievement scores can have negative side-effects such as narrowing the curriculum that is taught or wearing people out as they focus on the targets".

The OISE team found several of these negative side-effects, what they call 'Unintended Costs and Consequences', and their report points out some of the problems which have resulted from the current sharp focus on targets at all levels of the English educational system.

Small-scale successes

This pressure to force up scores is failing at a national level as far as boys are concerned; overall their scores continue to lag obstinately behind those of girls in reading and in writing. There are however a growing number of successful small-scale initiatives which are succeeding in raising boys' achievement. They are being reported locally, at INSET meetings, within local education authorities, on the Internet, and in publications like this one. These initiatives are undertaken by individual schools or teachers, and sometimes by LEAs. Some of

In several cases teachers in these classes seem to have succeeded in creating a classroom culture which is stronger than the peer group cultures that sometimes prevent boys from engaging fully in school literacy activities.

the features that they may have in common include:

- an emphasis on raising awareness among teachers, pupils and parents about the issues involved in boys' progress in literacy, with the focus always on improving expectations;

- the promotion of formal or informal networks which can support boys' literacy learning (eg reading clubs; reading and writing partners; reading mentors);

- the encouragement of more reflective approaches to reading and writing through the use of reading and writing journals;

- the use of more 'social' approaches to teaching literacy (eg literature circles) which boys have been observed to enjoy;

- an increased emphasis on ICT in teaching literacy;

- a recognition of boys' interest in using graphics; increased opportunities for planning writing through drawing, making diagrams and mental maps;

- the development of home-school links to support boys' literacy learning at home and at school.

Through these kinds of local initiatives schools and individual teachers are demonstrating that high expectations, stimulating teaching and appropriate support can help boys to make better progress in literacy. What many of these ways forward have in common is a readiness to attend to how children learn and to enable them to learn most effectively. To do this, the teachers involved have to be prepared to observe learners, and to be aware of them both as members of particular groups, but also as individuals who may not conform to routine expectations about 'what works for boys'.

In several cases teachers in these classes seem to have succeeded in creating a classroom culture which is stronger than the peer group cultures that sometimes prevent boys from engaging fully in school literacy activities. They have made it acceptable, even prestigious, for boys to be good at reading and writing.

Often linked to this has been the growing realisation that talk, or speaking and listening, is the foundation of all literacy learning, and that it has been neglected in some classrooms. Talk is a crucial halfway house in writing. Oral rehearsal - talking through an idea for a piece of writing, or simply telling someone what you are going to write in a kind of oral draft – can be one of the most helpful ways for an inexperienced writer to get started on a piece of writing. Many teachers have helped boys to improve their writing through a conscious focus on discussion and on talk for writing.

And drama, one of the most popular yet neglected oral language activities, can have an equally powerful influence on children's writing. The CLPE research on the influence of literature on children's writing found that one of the most important interventions made during the project was a single drama session based on *The Green Children*, one of the texts studied by all the schools involved. The after effects of this drama session were felt throughout the project year. Following the drama, children's writing was more detailed and fully imagined and they wrote in role confidently. The roots of writing, as Vygotsky stressed, lie in the other forms of symbolising (drawing, modelling, play, drama) that children engage in before they come to the abstract symbolic system of writing. Children who find writing difficult may be helped by using these more concrete forms of imagining as ways into writing.

Myra Barrs
CLPE

References

Aiken, Joan (1966) *Night Birds on Nantucket* London, Jonathan Cape

Barrs, Myra (1988) 'Maps of Play' in Meek, Margaret and Mills, Colin, eds. *Language and Literacy in the Primary School* London, Falmer Press

Barrs, Myra and Cork, Valerie (2001) *The Reader in the Writer* London, CLPE

Barrs, Myra and Pidgeon, Sue, eds (1998) *Boys and Reading* London, CLPE

Boyle, David (2001) *The Tyranny of Numbers: Why Counting Won't Make Us Happy* London, HarperCollins

Branford, Henrietta (1997) *Fire, Bed and Bone* London, Walker

Crossley-Holland, Kevin (1994) *The Green Children* Oxford University Press

Department for Education and Employment (2000) *The National Literacy Strategy. Grammar for Writing* London, DfEE

Fullan, Michael et al, Institute for Studies in Education, University of Toronto (2001) *Watching & Learning 2. OISE/UT Evaluation of the Implementation of the National Literacy and Numeracy Strategies. Second Annual Report* London, DfES

Hurston, Zora (1986) *Dust Tracks on a Road* London, Virago
[previous edition Philadelphia, Lippincott 1942]

Meek, Margaret (1988) *How Texts Teach What Readers Learn* Stroud, Thimble Press

Millard, Elaine (1997) *Differently Literate – boys, girls, and the schooling of literacy* London, Falmer Press

Moss, Gemma (1998) *The Fact and Fiction Research Project. Interim Findings* Southampton, University of Southampton Centre for Language in Education

NFER. *Progress in International Reading Literacy Survey* (PIRLS). Ongoing study disseminated through NFER.

Olson, David (1996) *The World on Paper. The conceptual and cognitive implications of writing and reading* Cambridge University Press

Peterson, Shelley (2001) University of Toronto

Vygotsky, Lev (1978) *Mind in Society: the Development of Higher Psychological Processes* Cambridge, Ma., Harvard University Press

Conseil Superieur de l'Education in Quebec report
http://www.cse.gouv.qc.ca/e/pub/avis/facteu_s.htm

CHAPTER 3

A story-telling project

Mary Jo McPherson

Storytelling demonstrates the pleasures of story writing and develops a sense of audience. In an action research project with a Year 5 class, a head teacher found that storytelling developed children's ability to imagine and empathise and enhanced the quality of their writing.

School Context

I am the headteacher at a three form entry Junior School in Lewisham, London. All year groups in the school have a weekly Arts Afternoon. Three classes are split between four teachers and children follow a block of arts-related work during which they can rotate through music, art, drama, dance and other arts activities. Sometimes these activities are linked to each other and to the ongoing class project.

For the purposes of the 'Boys and Writing' project I elected to do storytelling with a group of year 5 pupils, and to relate art and writing to the story. As well as the time on the Arts Afternoon, I had further access to one of the classes involved during literacy hours, at a time when story was the curriculum focus.

I was looking at boys generally, but in particular at James, who is at stage 2 on the SEN register. His writing is still at level 2, varying between 2C and 2B. He had been writing very short pieces, and his writing was sometimes quite unrelated to the task. I wanted to improve his speaking and listening, to extend his writing, to enable him to write with a better sense of structure, and to improve his capacity for imaginative expression.

Why Story?

I wanted to develop storytelling in its own right but also to use it as a way into narrative writing in general. Boys' narrative writing in our school reflects the national weakness in this area and like other teachers we sometimes question why we should expect children to be good story writers. It is a difficult art form at which most adults would fail. In the context of national assessment teachers can feel pressured into drilling children in techniques that gain marks. This kind of teaching misses the benefits that

> Since children, especially boys, can be more successful in other genres (which are also easier to teach), there is always the temptation to steer away from story

come from working with story.

Since children, especially boys, can be more successful in other genres (which are also easier to teach), there is always the temptation to steer away from story. Yet story reading and writing allows children to explore meanings and understand experience. Although the National Literacy Strategy recognises this, there can be such an obsession with the teaching of techniques that the real value of story can be overlooked.

I chose story for the following reasons:

- Everyone likes a story;
- I strongly believe that boys need to be exposed to more fiction, and introduced to fictions that they might not otherwise find for themselves;
- Boys in particular may need to develop their abilities to explore relationships, to understand the inner life of characters and to consider motivation. This is true of all children of course, and does not mean that boys are not already developing their own imaginative inner lives – but some may need to be given more time to reflect and discuss issues like these within a shared framework.

Why storytelling rather than story reading?

Storytelling is part of everyday life and is central to communication. Children experience story in many forms, including talk about their own experiences. Children need to be confident to express themselves; learning to tell stories in a way which will engage the interest of other people is an important learning experience for them.

Story today comes to children primarily

through film, TV and video. Here the quick succession of images leaves little space for children's own imaginations to operate creatively. They watch a lot but have little time for reflection. When they do talk about what they watch with peers ("*Did you see the bit where...?*") they recall the same episode, describing a remembered image in spoken language. This kind of talk uses memory and language skills but not necessarily creative thought. They have not created their own images – the story has been visualised for them.

And of course story can also be experienced through written fiction – if children seek such fictions and can overcome the hurdles of reading. But they have to set aside TV and computer games to engage in this reading and many of them, especially boys, are increasingly disinclined to do so.

I believed storytelling might help children to see the point of fiction, would involve them in the pleasures of story, and could also help them to become more interested in story reading and story writing.

A sense of audience

I also chose story telling to develop:

- an awareness in children of themselves as the audience for a story
- a sense of others as *their* audience during their own storytelling.

Children's awareness of the way in which they themselves operate as an active audience needs to be developed. If children are to sense and value their own imaginations at work, we have to draw out and value the different impressions that are created in different minds in response to a storyteller's words. Feelings have to be talked through. Different points of view have to be respectfully discussed. There has to be trust. If these opportunities are available, story can be an important means of developing awareness of the self and others.

The awareness of an audience also helps the teller. To be a storyteller, either to another pupil, to a group or to one's own family is a challenge for any child, and they can be helped towards it in little steps. Children have to learn to recreate the story, adding new elements from their imagination and presenting these to listeners who respond to them in their own way. Tellers have to think about their intentions, what they want to say – they have to become authors of the story.

Storytelling makes more explicit for children this important element of story writing that we try to teach – *a sense of audience*. They cannot avoid a sense of audience; the audience is present and the teller has to keep them on board. If I tell a story, I want you to listen. And to be listened to gives a boost to anyone's self-confidence. The response from the audience

helps the teller and is easy to see. By contrast, the audience for a child's written work may seem distant – it may well be a lone teacher.

Following the planned work on storytelling, I wanted to move the children into writing the story. The telling would be the springboard into writing, bridging the gap between the ideas in the head and the more formally structured writing process.

The teacher as storyteller

There are many useful exercises that can be used to induct children into the elements of story telling. However, teachers will not be able to facilitate storytelling for children if they have not devoted time to developing their own oral storytelling. Telling a story is very different from reading one. It needs more preparation and it requires the teller to be totally engaged.

As part of this preparation, storytellers silently rehearse their story. They may visualise the landscapes and the characters and listen to the voices. They always imbue a story with their own personal recollections, and perhaps with images from other stories, from films or other sources. The process of rehearsal makes the story familiar. Listening to their inner voice, they begin to respond emotionally to the story's content – to its conflicts or challenges.

This shaping of a story for a telling, even if it is not one's own story, is a very creative process. It allows us to explore our experience of the world. It develops a stronger sense of self and of others. Good storytelling is not merely a re-telling of another storyteller's plot. A well chosen story may teach children about structure, but most importantly it will contribute to their personal development.

Storytelling makes more explicit for children this important element of story writing that we try to teach – a sense of audience.

Story 1: The Clay Pot Boy

I began this project thinking that by developing storytelling skills I would also be able to develop stronger writing skills in children. To instil confidence in these inexperienced storytellers, I started with a very simple story – The Clay Pot Boy, in the version by Cynthia Jameson. This is a cumulative winding and unwinding story and could be used with younger children, as its shape supports memory. It has plenty of opportunities for audience participation, which helps the teller. It also involves voice changes and acting out *in situ*.

After the first telling everyone was keen to retell it. I said they could do this after the next exercise. I then asked them to spread themselves around the library carpet, lying comfortably in a space by themselves with their eyes closed and to 'walk around the story'. By this I explained that I meant them to imagine seeing this story unfold, following the character through the landscape, taking care to look around as they did so. They were to open their eyes when they had come to the end of the story.

To start them off I spoke an introduction from which they could continue. They all fell totally silent, with eyes closed, for approximately fifteen minutes. Then I asked them to form pairs and one of the pair started retelling the story. They were encouraged to help their partner by joining in or by adding actions. After a short time I asked them to swap roles.

All of the children took part enthusiastically. Before our next sessions I asked them to do two things:

i) to tell the Clay Pot Boy story to someone else e.g. a younger sibling

ii) to choose, with a partner, a different character which they would 'plant' in a similar story, of their own making.

At the next session they worked orally in pairs, building their cumulative tale and unwinding it. All then silently 'walked' their new story as before, in preparation for telling their story, working in pairs, to the whole group. James contributed a very well received individual story, which used Power Rangers as characters. I told him he was a born storyteller. Following this session, the stories were told to small groups of year 3 pupils, during a year 3 Arts Afternoon.

Story 2 : The Fisherman and The Mermaid

The next sessions involved a different story and was intended to lead to writing. I wanted the children to achieve written work with some of the following qualities:

• a good structure

> I then asked them to spread themselves around the library carpet, lying comfortably in a space by themselves with their eyes closed and to 'walk around the story'.

• some evidence that they were visualising the narrative

• evident empathy with the characters and reflection on the content of the story

• more use of complex sentences.

I chose a traditional folk tale: *The Fisherman and the Mermaid*. This is a 'Selkie' story of a fisherman who meets a mermaid and hides her magic garment in the thatched roof of his cottage in order to keep her on land. She lives seemingly happily with him for years, has children but always longs for the sea. Eventually she finds the cloth, leaves him and her children in the night and goes back to sea, never to be seen again.

This is a story with a well defined landscape and places for the imagination to roam. It has pace, without being 'action packed'. It also has abundant opportunities to explore the inner life of characters, to share their feelings of loneliness, kindness, family happiness, longing, separation, betrayal and blame. There are questions for the children to ask: Was the fisherman right to take the mermaid's magic garment? Was she right to leave her children?

Before telling the story I explained the significance of a mermaid's magic garment – she cannot return to the sea without it.

Session 1:
To experience the story and raise children's awareness of imagination at work

- Tell the story

  As always, it is important to tell the story as well as possible, visualising the seashore scenes and bringing out the strong feelings and the dilemmas that the characters experience.

- Ask children to share key points and images that they have imagined clearly.

  They can do this in pairs initially, and then share their imaginings with the whole group.

- Make clear to them that we all imagine things differently and that what we imagine is related to our experience.

  This is a very important area for discussion. It highlights how imagination is always at work and values each child's version of the story.

- Collect nine or ten key points that need to be included in a retelling of the story.

  This can be done as a list or on a wheel so that if they leave out something it can be inserted in the cycle.

Session 2:
An art session to stimulate visual imagination

- I wanted to develop children's powers of visualisation by asking them to translate their visual imaginings into a piece of art.

  In the classroom the children are asked to visualise any part of the story – the fisherman, the beach, the sea, the cloth, the cottage. They spend five minutes doing this, eyes closed.

- After this, it is helpful if the teacher models the activity, creating an image with the help of water-based crayons.

  The children use water based large crayons with large sheets of paper to create an abstract image that suggests key elements of their visualisation.

- They write a short description explaining their picture.

In this session, some children worked individually, though most chose to work with a partner. The decisions that took place around joint pictures involved good language and negotiation skills. I avoided asking children to draw, preferring them to concentrate on creating an impression using colour and line. Their art work was bold and colourful and their pieces of writing were vivid and thoughtful.

Here is one example from a pair of boys who wrote about the mermaid's garment:

It is a lovely cloth. He was hypnotised by it. It looked like twisty and turny purple and green, sparkingly magical. It had blue scales and light glimmering through its threads and the sea's waves with the sun on them

Hassan

The children's art work and their writing was displayed around the classroom to demonstrate the richness of everyone's imagination.

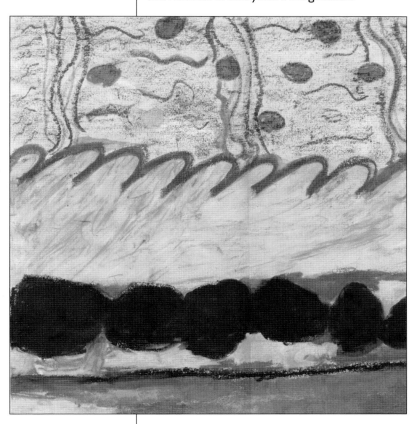

Session 3:
To prepare for telling by internalising the story

In this session we created a large class story-wheel that showed the plot but which also had on it key parts of the story that could be visualised. Several elements that were included in the wheel had already been explored by the children in their art work. Each pupil was asked to choose a few that they would like to focus upon.

In the library they carried out the mental 'walk your story' exercise individually. They knew they did not have to describe everything – some things should be left to the listeners' imaginations, even if they themselves could see the story clearly. We had our first re-telling from one child. Quite naturally he gave a detailed and imaginative retelling of the part he had explored in his artwork. After this session, children were asked to tell the story to someone at home.

> They knew they did not have to describe everything – some things should be left to the listeners' imaginations

As yet there had been no reference to the fisherman's motives except by a boy who said he thought he was a bit evil. I put this opinion to the class. Generally their sympathies lay with the fisherman. They felt he should be excused for what he had done because of his loneliness. We talked about their own experience of loneliness. These are some of the things they said in the discussion:

'It's like when you have nobody to play with on a Saturday afternoon.'

'It's like when you are sent to your room and you have been there ages and nobody comes to get you.'

'It's like when you are in bed and the pillow's wet and then it's all cold and you can't get to sleep.'

'It's like somebody you like doesn't like you any more and they're going round with other people and they're happy and you're not.'

'It's like being the last hamster left in the cage and the rest have all died.'

'It feels like a sharp gun shot and a bullet going through your heart'.

Everybody liked this last suggestion, which was made by a boy. And would these feelings excuse doing wrong to others? I asked them.

Generally the children excused small wrongs which were delivered without intent to hurt. The fisherman was forgiven for what he had done to the mermaid, but the children suggested that he should have gone to visit another fisherman instead and been content to live alone. Many were aware that the fisherman's taking of the cloth led from unhappiness to a long period of happiness and then to sadness again for him. They knew that

We moved into writing through the use of mind maps to produce small chunks of descriptive writing. These maps were used to construct simple sentences which were then combined into more complex sentences.

The children had just been introduced to mind maps as a way of organising their thinking. However, some of their efforts here are really 'brainstorms'. The objective here is to move methodically from disjointed ideas about the key elements, to prioritising these in a logical way and discarding the superfluous ones. Children need to be aware of thinking processes as positive logical steps, not confusion.

James used his mind-map to write about the mermaid's garment:

The fisherman looked at the garment. It was a masterpiece of art and it made the sun shine brightly. It had all the lovely colours of the swaying seas blue green white and purple. It would take away all your darkness inside

And here is using his mind-map to write about the beach:

The calm beach of tranquility was as beautiful as ever. The waves crashed on the rocks and the seagulls were flying. It was so peaceful. It felt like a place to pray. It was a place to go if you had something on your mind. The fisherman went there quite often. He was lonely and he longed for a wife and children.

James had been helped to organise these sentences by his response partner. No one else had written or said anything like this. His description conjures up aloneness and creates a serious mood. It was set aside for future use.

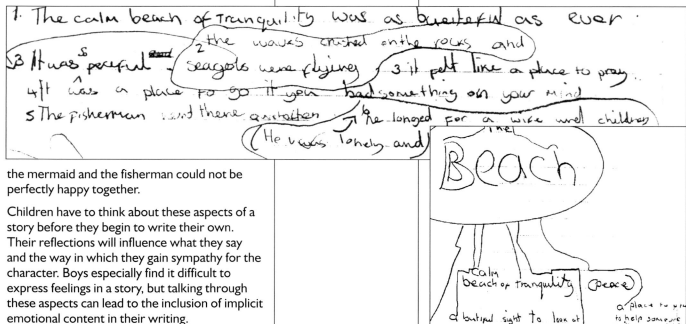

the mermaid and the fisherman could not be perfectly happy together.

Children have to think about these aspects of a story before they begin to write their own. Their reflections will influence what they say and the way in which they gain sympathy for the character. Boys especially find it difficult to express feelings in a story, but talking through these aspects can lead to the inclusion of implicit emotional content in their writing.

Session 6:
Writing

Having explored and responded to the story the children wrote their own versions. They used mind-maps to support the writing by adding detail at key points. James set about his work confidently and wrote the following piece of story.

Once upon a time there lived a fisherman and he longed for a wife. He lived on the end of a cliff. He had a house with a thatched roof and whitewash. Sometimes he goes out but ends up turning back, sometimes he used to walk down on the calm beach of tranquillity. Tonight it was as beautiful as ever. It was peaceful. The waves crashed upon this beach slapping the wet rocks. The sea gulls flew over. It felt like the perfect place to pray. He often went there to get things off his mind. This night he went to the beach and he heard the most beautiful singing he had ever heard. He followed the sound. Soon he came across a mermaid singing. His heart was pounding. The mermaid's face was enchanted with beauty and her smooth black hair and her lovely green and blue scales glowed in the dark. The fisherman gasped because she was so beautiful. He sneaked up upon her and took the garment. He ran and ran and ran until he could run no more. Before you know it she's at the house. Inside the fisherman was looking at the garment. He is hypnotised because it is so beautiful. It was a work of art. The fisherman hid it under the thatch where no one can find it. It was the first time she had ever seen a fire. It was the the first time she had ever seen a chair nice and comfortable it was she was amazed. She stayed with the fisherman and they got married

This section of a story uses the description of the beach and mermaid from his mind maps, but James has omitted to describe his cloth. However, he uses his cloth description later in the story.

The little boy stepped out of the bath. He turned to his mother in excitement shouting "Mum, mum, guess what I saw today. I saw the most beautiful cloth. It fell from the thatch. The sun shone in it. It has all the colours of the sea, green blue white and purple. It would take away all your darkness inside. She was filled with shock. She was happy and full of sadness. Both.

When James came to describe the mermaid going back to the water he used the text that he had written alongside his artwork, the picture of the mermaid returning to the sea:

She felt sorrowful. She was burning up inside. She left her children sleeping and went down the cliff path. She stood on the beach and the mountains were in the background. The waves came up to her feet on the sand and the tangled seaweed swallowed around. The moon was glimmering on the water. The beautiful mermaid wrapped her cloth around her and leapt into the waves.

The quality of the imagining in this story was impressive.

> Working with storytelling has visibly helped Sean to extend the amount and quality of his work. It has helped all the group in a similar way.

Further Reading

Barton, Bob & Booth, David (1990) *Stories in the Classroom* Pembroke Publishing
Livo, Norma J & Reitz, Sandra (1984) *Storytelling Process and Practice* Libraries Unlimited

Conclusions

Working with storytelling has visibly helped James to extend the amount and quality of his work. It has helped all the group in a similar way.

The project also developed children's speaking and listening skills. Reflection time, with the opportunity to rehearse a story in one's mind without fear of failure, gave them confidence. Children became more aware of the inner voice which organises thought. For some children, their use of expression, gesture, eye contact and voice change in their storytelling were suggestive of a growing awareness of audience.

Their writing was well supported within the clear framework of the familiar story. The steps of the process, from listening, to thinking, to speaking, to visualising, to writing were guided. Mind-maps broke down the stages of the story so that writing could initially be done in small, successful chunks. The story also generated art work and related talk, all of which supported descriptive writing. The quality of the boys' descriptive writing in this project was on a par with that of the girls.

The whole class developed their ability to empathise and express this feeling of empathy both explicitly and implicitly. Most importantly, they enjoyed the whole unit of work. It was a social activity with lots of peer support and opportunities to perform. They were able to bring their new skills into their own home by telling stories to siblings and parents.

A storytelling project like this is a multi-sensory experience that will develop children as speakers, readers and writers, if embedded in school practice. At my school we are beginning to use storytellers more often and to use them more productively. We have a Year 3 after-school storytellers' club and two small Year 4 lunch-time reading and storytelling groups. Our Year 5 will do some extended work with a storyteller in the spring. Staff have had INSET led by a storyteller.

We need to further develop our own skills in storytelling. We also need to work with parents to raise the value of this important medium by encouraging them to be tellers and audience for their children. Above all as a school we need to endlessly provide audiences for story and writing through response partners, class books, story performance, assemblies, and school magazines.

Mary Jo McPherson, Torridon Junior School, London Borough of Lewisham

References

Jameson, Cynthia (1973) *The Clay Pot Boy* New York, Putnam Publishing Co.
Rosen, Betty (1991) *Shapers and Polishers. Teachers as Storytellers* London, Mary Glasgow Publications
This book gives twelve stories to work with, including 'The Fisherman and the Mermaid'

Can drama and role-play help boys with writing? This case study shows that introducing a range of drama and video into literacy lessons helped improve both the quality of the writing and the boys' enjoyment of the writing process.

It makes you feel like you are there!

Using drama and video to extend writing

Sue Bown

Why is writing such a problem for boys? Do they dislike putting pen to paper or does a lack of basic skills, a lack of imagination or a lack of stimulation have a part to play? This was a question I had asked myself as a teacher, over a number of years. The Boys and Writing course gave me the opportunity to think about these questions and made me further determined to follow them up

Evidence from early years teachers would suggest that boys and girls both enjoy early writing experiences and incorporate 'play' writing into many of their role-play activities. Do we need to extend this form of role-play and look for more opportunities to include early writing in play? If there is enjoyment of writing by both boys and girls at foundation level, when does the gap between boys and girls' writing begin to appear?

There is no doubt, that in the main, girls settle down to tasks earlier than boys as schooling becomes more formal; they settle better to 'school learning'. They tend to be more eager to please, more willing to participate in teacher-generated activities, less excitable and generally better behaved. There is maybe a need to investigate how far home expectations differ with regard to girls and boys and whether maturity plays a significant part as boys and girls grow up. Does peer pressure itself contribute to the way boys evaluate literacy, and writing in particular? Does the inherent make-up and differences between boys and girls contribute to growing differences?

Attainment

It is noticeable in our school that the difference in the attainment of boys and girls in reading and writing is very slight at the end of KS1. Year 2000 results showed the number of boys at NC

Does peer pressure itself contribute to the way boys evaluate literacy, and writing in particular? Does the inherent make-up and differences between boys and girls contribute to growing differences?

level 2 and above in reading to be 41 and the girls 42. In writing the results were boys 37, girls 41, from a year group of 46 boys and 44 girls. Results are slightly above the national average.

Yet at the end of KS2 there is a significant difference between the boys and girls. Why? Can we redress the balance and stimulate writing for all, but particularly for the boys? And if we can improve all, can the boys make a more dramatic step forward to narrow the gap? Can we construct an exciting climate where it is 'cool' to succeed, where writing is fun and successful? There is no doubt that the NLS is helping to achieve higher results but the gap between boys and girls is still there because the girls are also improving.

I had been particularly interested on the project in the session and subsequent discussions about how role-play, video and drama can support

writing. I began to focus my questions towards this. Can drama and role-play help to stimulate vocabulary and develop empathy for characters in writing? Can using video and drama help to improve the quality of writing? These were the questions and issues in my mind as I set about identifying a group of boys to focus on for my work on the Boys and Writing project

Initially I decided to study four boys from my literacy group who are also in my class, and they have remained the mainstay of my research, although I have used examples from others. I teach the top literacy set in Year 5, a group of twenty four children where the girls outnumber the boys quite significantly. The boys I chose presented themselves in class as the 'can and don'ts', and, although able, lacked apparent interest in writing. Their overall Year 4 SATs results were as follows: -

Michael	3a
Clive	3b
Terry	3b
Stephen (new to school in September)	

How the boys feel about writing

The first thing I did was to ask the boys for their feelings about 'writing' and was quite surprised at some of the responses.

"I don't like writing because it's boring."

"I like writing some short stories sometimes when I see birds and things. I like writing about animals."

"I quite like writing especially stories and recounts and stuff like that because they are from things to write. You can imagine the things."

"I like writing stories because it's fun imagining up stuff."

"I quite like writing. It's fun. Writing journals

> Can drama and role-play help to stimulate vocabulary and develop empathy for characters in writing? Can using video and drama help to improve the quality of writing?

help me with my literacy work. I can practise in my book and it doesn't matter if it's not quite right. I can go over and over."

"Alright. I like writing stories best because I can write more – I enjoy extended writing – I prefer a longer time to write more rather than short sessions."

"I like it. It's fun, especially journals."

"Alright – I don't like it that much."

I was surprised that so many of the boys actually said that they liked writing but the writing journals which we introduced in September to Year 5 have proved to be very popular with most of the children. They feel that they have the freedom to write what they want to. Writing journals are definitely helping to practise their skills in different genres without the limitations of working on anything in particular or worrying about getting things wrong.

I wanted to go on and ask them to reflect more on the successful writing and so asked what helped them with their writing?

"Thinking in my head – imagining – thinking through."

"Think of a good idea out of a story that I've read. Like to use a bit of it to develop ideas or change them around."

"I think of a beginning based on the title."

"If I have an idea in my head. Teachers say – do whatever you think of."

It also seems that the boys like the time to expand their ideas, so while the short sessions are beneficial and essential for teaching skills, I have found in Year 5 that they appreciate the extended literacy writing time to get to grips with their writing and to work on their journals. They do like a good stimulus. It helps to get them started, to get a clear picture in their head on which to build.

Drama, role-play and videos

My focus for trying to improve boys' writing was to introduce a drama or role-play stimulus at the beginning of the lesson. I have done this in a number of ways and as a result now plan to use drama and video as a regular strategy in my teaching of writing.

I have used drama and video in three different ways:
- I have set up situations where the whole class can act out a part of a scene first, to really get into character before writing.

- I have arranged for a group of children to prepare a scene to act out in front of the class. This provided the initial stimulus for the class to write.

- I have used extracts from videos to set the scene at the beginning of a story, or get straight in to the action. The very visual impact has helped the children to quickly orientate themselves to the story.

My experience using drama and videos on this project has made me much more aware of their potential in supporting writing in specific and different ways. I plan to continue to work in this way so, for example, when we look at persuasive writing in the summer term, I will ask the children to take on roles in a dispute, for example farmers, councillors, householders, and act out their position in the dispute before putting pen to paper. I will also use video when we do an in-depth study of *Tom's Midnight Garden* by Philippa Pearce.

Whole class drama stimulus

One of the first activities that I tried in September was some recount work. The class examined a fiction recount about Frankenstein at the point where the monster created wakes up. All the class acted the scenario out. They lay on the floor, tried to shut their ears to all sound, their eyes to all sights, then slowly pretended to wake and be aware of what they could see, hear and feel as they rose up. The writing that followed was very good. Most of the class got into role and included depth of feeling and empathy for the character in their written accounts.

Michael: *I opened my eyes. I saw lots of lights and there were lots of machines around me. Everything looked peculiar. I slowly sat up and looked around me. I saw someone jumping up and down, shouting hooray. I took a couple of steps forward and I wobbled because of how big I was. The man paused and said hello. I completely ignored him and walked over to the machine   and touched it and it fell over. The man went mad. I said sorry but that wasn't enough. He started shouting at me. He made me feel quite sad.*

Derek: *I open my eyes and life came into me. I could see all the blinding colours shoot into my eyes. I was alive. I put a smile on my face but then it went away because I was ugly so I blamed it on my creator Dr. Frankenstein. I was not glad to be alive.*

I felt that in this writing the boys had made a real effort to show empathy of character. For example with Terry's monster there is a feeling of confusion of not knowing what things are and great size – *'what's this thing tingling '* – *'I see a tiny creature in the corner'* and then the sadness of discovery that he is the ugly monster – *'I see no one but myself'* – *'could it mean me''* – *'I see a reflection of me. I am ashamed of myself. I am disgusting. I am a beast.'*

Michael also gives us the idea of size *'I wobbled because of how big I was' 'I walked over to the machine and touched it and it fell over'* and he

My experience using drama and videos on this project has made me much more aware of their potential in supporting writing in specific and different ways.

expresses the feelings of his character – *'I said sorry but that wasn't enough. He started shouting at me, he made me feel quite sad.'*

Small group scenario

Another strategy I tried out was to get a small group from the class to prepare a scene to act out. This has to be arranged the day before. We took the book *Step by Wicked Step* by Anne Fine and a mixed group of boys and girls acted out the opening chapter. This involved them pretending to be on a school trip to an old house. The school children in the story had been separated from the main coach party and were travelling on a mini-bus, arriving at the house late at night in a storm. The story was acted out until the group of school children find themselves in a tower room. The objective for the writing that followed was to write new scenes into a story. None of the children had read on so their continuation of the story was from their own imagination.

Michael: *Pixie got dressed and said to the others*

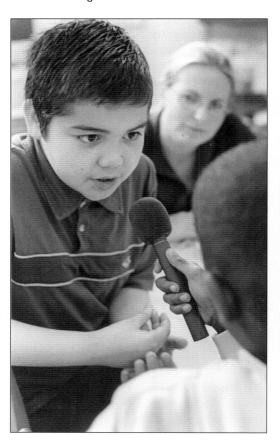

"Who's coming with me?" Robbo stuck his hand up and said, "I will come with you. Pixie got up off the bed and said let's go Robbo, so they slowly walked over to the door with the wooden floor creaking underneath them. They pushed the door open and it creaked. The others said we will stay here and wait for Mr. Plumley. Pixie and Robbo both took the step onto the stairs. Robbo said "I'm scared already." "Don't worry," said Pixie. They quickly trotted up the stairs as fast as they could. They were very windy. Suddenly they saw some light coming from around the corner. They slowed

down and started to creep the rest of the way, then they saw a door and saw a man sitting in his chair. Pixie said "that must be the house keeper." They went up to the door and knocked on it. The man turned and he had the most ugly face in the world. He stood up and pulled a knife out of his pocket.

Derek: Robbo looked around. It was gloomy and there were nine to twelve rats around the room. He went to a window. He could see lightning and a lot of trees. He then thought about what Pixie had said "this place is haunted." He also was cold then he thought maybe he should go through the door.

"Let's see what's beyond that door!" he said confidently. The girls shook their heads but Colin said "OK, I don't care." But the only thing was, were they going to die.

Robbo opened the door and he heard "When are we going to eat our prey?" The voice sounded like someone with a bad throat.

"Maybe we should go back" said Ralph frightened like a sissy girl. Claudia pushed him back. Then they went up the stairs and when they got to the top they saw a dead man with a sword and crossbow.

Ralph said, "These weapons are from the medieval ages."

The boys quite successfully built some atmosphere into their settings and have made an attempt at using improved vocabulary. Terry used expressions like 'cobwebs smudged over' and 'coffin shaped box'. Michael's character spoke in a 'shivery voice'. Billy used expressions like 'back down to earth' and 'the most ugly face in the world', while one of Clive's characters 'sounded like someone with a bad throat'.

Whole class drama from class novel

As we continued to look at the books of Anne Fine, we read *The Angel of Nitshill Road* which deals with the subject of bullying. Again we acted out some of the parts and characters. The following work was to take the character "Barry Hunter" – the school bully – to his home as an extended story writing exercise. Here are some parts from the stories.

Terry: *Click went the door as Barry came in. From where Barry was it looked a mess, clothes on the floor.*

"Hello dear," yelled his Mum from upstairs.

"Alright Mum", he called in a bored way. The sofa sank under Barry. With one flick of the remote the TV came on, Barry's favourite programme came on, The Simpsons. Click, his step dad came in.

"Get up and do your jobs." he ordered like a soldier.

"But Mike," he said miserably.

> The boys quite successfully built some atmosphere into their settings and have made an attempt at using improved vocabulary.

> Terry used expressions like 'cobwebs smudged over' and 'coffin shaped box'. Michael's character spoke in a 'shivery voice'.

"No buts" ordered Mike simply, "go and start on your room." Clunk, clunk went Barry on the stairs. He sat on his bed looking at the clothes and stuff all over the floor."

Stephen: *Barry walked in the house and slammed the door furiously then he heard a stern voice from the kitchen.*

"Barry!" So Barry walked into the room and his mum gave him one of those looks.
"Barry what do you think this book is? Hmm hmm." Barry didn't want to answer because he knew what it was. It was the book that Celeste had given Mr. Fairway.

"So, thought about it yet?

"Yes." replied Barry nervously.

"Oh, so you do and guess something else."

"W.w..w..w…wh…what?" Barry was shivering like a leaf and the hairs on his back were on end. He knew something was going to happen.

"YOU'RE GROUNDED FOR TWO MONTHS!" Barry's mum boomed so loud he almost flew back and hit the wall. Barry went up to his room, he slammed the door so hard it almost went off the hinges and then he started trashing the room like he was mental.

"It's not fair!" Barry roared and screeched and yelled, trashing his room till it looked like a bomb and tornado had gone through it."

The boys really developed the character of Barry Hunter as they took him home. We saw another side of him from the bully that we had read about at school and a very realistic situation emerged. In Terry's story we find out that Barry is the victim of a bullying stepfather so when he is told to do his jobs ('ordered like a soldier'), the reply is 'But Mike,' he said miserably'.

Stephen sees the mother as the one in control in his story and so the character of Barry at home is in complete contrast to the bully at school. So Stephen has Barry 'shivering like a leaf and the hairs on his back on end' but it doesn't stop him from going upstairs and 'trashing his room till it looked like a bomb and tornado had gone through it.'

Using Videos

Another way that I tried to stimulate the boys' writing was to use part of a video as a starter. For example the children did a week's work based on the Titanic and as part of that we used an extract from the video. We used this as a starting point for diary and story writing. With hindsight I think it would have been beneficial to have two videos of the Titanic with one part showing the luxury near the beginning of the film and another extract showing the disaster at the end. The objective for the writing that followed was to write a recount in diary format.

Michael: *Saturday – I was walking on the top deck looking at the lovely bright colourful sea and eating a chocolate bar. In the sea I saw some lovely dolphins, they were beautiful swimming about like a fairy flying in the air. I walked over to the ball and went inside and sat down to have a drink of shandy. After that I went to have a dance. It was the best ever boat I have ever been on. It's not going to sink so I am completely safe.*

Sunday – I woke up on Sunday morning and got out of bed. I could hardly walk. I crawled over to my suitcase and opened it very slowly and dressed. When I was dressed, I stumbled out of the door and hurt my leg. It was only a little bruise though. I walked over to the middle deck and there was a lot of water in there and we started sinking. I was frightened, terrified. Every lifeboat had gone so I dived in and swam to a boat. I was safe.

The boys have tried to build up the contrast between the before and after of the Titanic sinking, how luxurious the journey was before and the distress and devastation afterwards. In his writing Terry conveys his characters' despair. He starts Monday with *'I can't believe it, they said it was unsinkable but that iceberg tore up the side and it went down'* and with questioning *'why didn't I die with my wife and child? Why has God forsaken us? I hate myself.'*

From the diary they went on to write a recount in story form. The story recount was to follow on from the moment of the crash. Writing in the first person Michael gives a good description from the viewpoint of his character rushing to escape and then *'sitting on the lifeboat watching people die' 'we could hear them screaming' 'people falling down the hole. It was horrendous!'* He slows the pace down with a feeling of his character's despair: *'Later help arrived but all they found was dead bodies and rubble. They picked us up and I just looked back at the horror and knowing that I will never forget the beautiful Titanic.'*

Clive shows empathy for his character in the feeling of panic and rushing to escape that comes through in his writing as his character *'tried to get to the top'* and *'ran through the water hoping I wouldn't drown' ' running out of breath'. 'I needed to stop or I'd get a heart attack but I couldn't stop. It was either stop and drown or run and live.'* Clive, like Michael, also slows down the pace towards the end with *'I then started to row away in the life boat slowly, very slowly.'*

Stephen also uses questions to get into his character: *'I was forced to get a life jacket on and go to top deck. I had been told that there was nothing to worry about but if there wasn't anything to worry about why did I have to wear a life jacket if everything was supposable alright?'* And again the distress and despair of his character comes out in *'I could see people clinging for their lives. The horror in their eyes! They were trying to hold back their fear and*

I asked the boys if it helped their writing to have a video or drama starter for writing and they were universal in their agreement

---

then the ship went down.' 'Later help arrived but it was too late. It was gone, all gone and I felt guilty because I survived.'

Terry chose to write with Jim, a member of the crew, as his character and chose dramatic language to get his message across starting *'The cold air was making Jim shiver. A couple of people were playing with the ice. The damage was too much for the ship. Now they knew the truth, the Titanic was sinkable as they found out'*. Terry moves the action along and then reaches the climax, *'The aft lifted vertically in the air and started to go down. Jim jumped into the freezing water. Jim felt like he had been stabbed a thousand times.'* In Terry's story, Jim is not a survivor – *'the funnel was coming off there was no time for him to get away so he stayed still as the funnel took his life.'*

Can drama help?

From my research over the last few months, there is no doubt that using drama, role-play or videos as a starting point does help to stimulate vocabulary and empathy for characters in boys' writing. I asked the boys if it helped their writing to have a video or drama starter for writing and they were universal in their agreement

"Makes you feel like you're in it. I love acting – since I've been acting it makes me think more – everything is more realistic – easier to get the atmosphere – it helps me."

"Yes – you can get straight into action – imagine you are there."

"Yes, it helps when we have a starter on video. I can go straight into the action."

A recent assessment of my four boys showed that Terry and Clive are now working at level 4a and Michael and Stephen at level 4c, so progress had been made. More satisfactory to me though, is the fact that the boys are enjoying their writing, are confident writers and are much more able to show empathy for their characters in their writing while also experimenting with more exciting vocabulary. However the stimulation of drama has also improved the girls' writing to an equal extent and so the gap between the boys and girls is still there!

Sue Bown
Stifford Primary School, Thurrock

References

Fine, Anne (1992) *The Angel of Nitshill Road* London, Methuen
Fine, Anne (1995) *Step by Wicked Step* London, Hamish Hamilton
Pearce, Philippa (1958) *Tom's Midnight Garden* Oxford, Oxford University Press

IT MAKES YOU FEEL LIKE YOU ARE THERE!

CHAPTER 5

An aversion to writing

Elizabeth Baker

How can teachers work with secondary pupils who have developed a real aversion to writing? How can they prevent English from being labelled 'uncool'? A special school teacher seeks to understand the roots of one pupil's hostility to literacy, and relate what she observes to research in gender and literacy.

Introduction

The underachievement of boys compared to girls has become a matter of concern during recent years for all those involved in education in the UK. Much discussion and research has revolved around reading achievement. Statistics have shown some improvement in this area since the introduction of the NLS but now the key stage test results have focused our attention on the underachievement of boys in writing.

The following statistics set a context for the focus of this paper.

- In 1999 49% of 11 year old boys achieved the level of writing expected for their age, an increase of 4% on the previous year.

- 64% of girls achieved this level – an increase of 5% on the previous year.

- In 1999 at the end of Key Stage 3 the significant gender difference remained with 55% of boys in England achieving level 5 or above in comparison to 72% of girls.

- More boys than girls achieved no A-G passes at G.C.S.E. in1999.

- The vast majority of pupils who were permanently excluded from school in 1997/8 were boys.

- In 1998/9 2 out of 3 pupils in special schools were boys.

Source of Data, DfEE

This paper seeks to define and unpick the problems that boys with special educational needs have with writing and to suggest some ways that will encourage and motivate these boys to write.

Questions that have arisen in the course of the study that I undertook as part of the Boys and Writing project are:

- What count as writing in an S.E.N. context?

- How can we sustain the interest and application of boys with S.E.N. in writing?

- Are there ways of encouraging independent writing in these contexts?

- Do we sufficiently value the oral contributions of boys?

- What is it about English and Literacy in general which makes it uncool for so many boys?

I will be focusing on a group of pupils that as teachers we all know well. They are male, hostile to school culture, very reluctant to write, skilful at manipulating those around them and sometimes talented in another curriculum area or interest outside school. Elaine Millard (1997) describes them as:

"….A bottom set of difficult, truculent males who cannot wait to leave school and who spend much of their time in class confronting the system in the person of the teacher".

My opportunity, working in a special school setting, was to examine one of these pupils in depth. I wanted to look at his problems with writing and see if I could set up strategies to support him. Since inclusion is a major plank of the government's education policy, this issue becomes more and more relevant to mainstream schools, as they take on pupils previously educated in a special school context.

Case History: Paul

Paul was a pupil who fulfils all the criteria for my research. He came to our school when he was nine years old. His statement emphasises "Major problems with behaviour and literacy". He was assessed in English as working towards

> I will be focusing on a group of pupils that as teachers we all know well. They are male, hostile to school culture, very reluctant to write, skilful at manipulating those around them and sometimes talented in another curriculum area or interest outside school.

level 1. His teacher reported that:
"He can copy write. He has been working on producing an unaided sentence, but lacks motivation and becomes quickly frustrated,"

Her targets for him were:
"To increase concentration, develop listening skills, encourage turn taking, develop cooperation with peers."

His mother's input to the statement comments on Paul's difficulty with literacy and behaviour. She noted his ability at practical tasks, his enjoyment of life on the street and his excellent sense of direction. (This was just as well in view of his tendency to run off after 'wobblers' at school). She mentioned that, *"…he quickly becomes upset if he feels humiliated"*.

During Year 6 Paul was assessed by the occupational therapist because of difficulties with handwriting. The therapist reported that:
"His motor planning is good in some areas, but he has difficulty motor planning when copying, suggesting visual motor interaction problems. There is a lack of fluency in fine motor control. His letter formation is inconsistent."

Her recommendations were followed by a programme which Paul refused to carry out.

Because of his oral ability and obvious intelligence Paul was also put forward for an experimental one-to-one computer assisted programme for reading in Year 6. This began successfully, but Paul was reluctant to co-operate after a few lessons and the programme made little difference to his reading.

At the end of Year 6 Paul's teacher commented on his disappointing English results in view of his success in Maths and Science. She added that he was difficult to motivate in reading.

Paul's behaviour initially worsened on his transfer to the secondary department, but showed some improvement with the implementation of a behaviour programme. An external observer described him as:
"…an extremely demanding pupil who actively seeks to get off tasks by offering to do jobs, talking to TA whilst teacher or another pupil is talking to class… He monopolises and dominates group activities… He resents not being given attention immediately by adults… He reacts well to praise… He does not make eye contact with peers. He has no problem with adults… He occasionally shouts out "I can't read".

One of her recommendations was that he should have access to a Successmaker computer English package. Complicated arrangements were made for this. Paul attended twice at another centre and then his parents and Paul requested that this should cease.

At the end of Year 8 Paul was assessed as working within level 1 for writing. His end of year report stated that:

I was aware of his hostility to literacy and I would be responsible for his progress in English for the next three years.

"…he has improved listening skills in literacy. He tends to complain about doing written tasks, but eventually begins a task late."

His reading age was 7.3 on the Hertfordshire Reading Score. The English Targets from his I.E.P. were

- To write a short account, correctly punctuated.
- To be aware of whether a piece of writing is complete.
- To write a simple story.
- To write a story with a distinct beginning, middle and end.
- To write a poem.

I chose Paul as the basis for this research because he presented a problem to me at the start of the year. I had been involved with his behaviour problems for some years: I was aware of his hostility to literacy and I would be responsible for his progress in English for the next three years.

The case study

I teach Paul within a Year 9 class of 8 pupils with a wide range of Special Educational Needs. The class includes the following pupils:

3 pupils with severe language/hearing problems who are signing and using symbols to write.

1 pupil with physical and perceptual problems who needs technical and one-to-one help to write.

1 pupil with Downs Syndrome level 1/2 N.C.

1 pupil wheelchair bound with some visual problems, level 1/2 N.C.

1 pupil with language problems, level 1/2 N.C.

The class has five one-hour English lessons each week, two of which are organised as literacy hours. As I saw it, at the start of Year 9 Paul's problems with writing were as follows:

- a family background where there was a history of difficulties with literacy (his Dad had problems with reading and writing)
- a history of turbulence.
- difficulties with handwriting.
- extreme lack of confidence in his ability to spell, write, compose.
- well developed strategies to avoid writing.
- an over-dependence on the support of adults in his writing.
- lack of skill in spelling.
- lack of skill in organising his work.
- problems of attention and application.
- antagonism to writing.
- unwillingness to problem solve.

I felt sure that there were other, perhaps more

underlying, problems which I could not quite identify. During the course of my reading I began to have some perception of these and they became of increasing interest as the project developed.

Planned Intervention

I began by interviewing Paul and some other boys in the group on their writing. They all said that their mothers were the primary writers in the family. Paul claimed to prefer writing stories and poems. He found spelling, copying, handwriting and 'thinking of what to say' difficult. At home he preferred writing with his Mum's pen; at school he preferred writing on the computer because it was easier as you 'pressed buttons'.

Another boy gave some suggestions as to the help that teachers could give him: 'give me more time', 'let me write on the computer', and 'give me a bank of words'. This led to other pupils in the group making their own lists. Paul suggested: 'easier writing', 'practising spelling', 'bank of words with pictures next to them' and 'dictionary'.

My plan was to investigate different methods of motivating and supporting Paul within the class in a variety of literacy activities. I also aimed to assess my success in this and monitor his progress towards his targets over a three month period.

I planned a programme of writing experiences supported by the literacy hour. My aim was to persuade and challenge Paul to produce some independent writing. The topic for the term was 'Food' so most of the literacy activities were based around this. Paul was very skilled at avoiding writing activities and these sessions frequently resulted in a bout of bad behaviour, so I knew this would be an interesting term!

As I have tried to demonstrate, Paul appeared (from my own and other teachers' observations) to have a deep-seated aversion to writing. On the whole he behaved well in practical lessons. He performed well and exhibited some pleasure in his work. He was particularly interested in anything involving plants and animals. He had his own horse and was knowledgeable about horses and animals in general. His teachers had all built on this interest in school. He was initially interested in most new topics, confident orally and had recently become more confident in reading, when he was personally engaged in the reading material. (He did not perform well in a test situation and had made no progress, in terms of his reading age, for 18 months).

Paul had well developed strategies to avoid writing. These included: asking to go to the toilet as soon as a writing task was set; taking his time over finding a pen, pencil and ruler; mending the computer; manipulating the

teacher; disturbing other pupils; asking the Teaching Assistant to write for him; deleting his work from the computer; asking for spellings or dictionaries and then going to fetch them himself. If all else failed there was always the possibility of a tantrum so that he could avoid the task completely.

My plan was:

- to offer the class a variety of writing tasks and to monitor which ones Paul found most interesting and stimulating
- to provide a variety of supports in order to find out which he found most helpful
- to offer different stimuli

I wanted to see if I could change this aversion to writing in any way and channel it into something more constructive.

The writing activities I planned would include:

Lists, letters, stories, poems, booklets, sequencing exercises, observation and thinking exercises, invitations, questions, written comprehension answers on a text, reports, menus, speech, email.

The writing supports would include:

Word lists (on wall and in books), dictionaries, writing frames, modelling, shared writing, use of computer software, teaching of spelling, punctuation, high frequency words, initial letters, blends, rhyming, use of the word processor, spell checks, encouragement, teacher writing to pupil dictation (on occasion), collaborative writing.

The stimuli I was going to use would include:

James and the Giant Peach, Magic Mash (class Jet Book), *George's Marvellous Medicine*, recipe books, TV cookery programmes, information books, poetry, computer software, visits to a supermarket, food tasting, French party, an assembly to read and display work, use of the internet and email, choices of activity.

When I began to reflect on the activities, supports and stimuli that Paul responded to (detailed in the lesson accounts below) I was interested to note that in almost all cases he had shown some interest in some part of the lesson. He was nearly always listening. And although he was often shouting out at inappropriate times, he was often first with an idea, answer, spelling or solution. He often asked to read (particularly the speech bubbles which he could read as exclamations). He very quickly got the gist of a story or poem and was able to predict or suggest outcomes.

When I examined the activities that Paul had been offered, he had almost always attempted each task. His main aim, however, was to finish as quickly as possible. He had no pride in his

Paul was very skilled at avoiding writing activities and these sessions frequently resulted in a bout of bad behaviour, so I knew this would be an interesting term!

work and often deleted, destroyed or lost it before I could save it. He showed initial interest in the oral and reading part of the lesson, but gave up as soon as writing was involved. He failed to use the supports that were given to him, not wanting to do anything which involved searching, finding, or sustaining his concentration. When oral tasks were involved, the story was different.

Literacy lessons

A pair of literacy lessons illustrates this well. The aim of the first lesson was for pupils to understand the layout of a recipe and to write their own simple recipe with supports (writing frame, example, word list, adult support).

A recipe for a sandwich was shown, discussed, read and rehearsed. Pupils were asked to write their own sandwich recipe using word lists around the room. Paul began to complete the frame using the illustration. He found it difficult and began to grow truculent. I sat next to him, encouraged and supported him and tried to persuade him to write. He tried a little, then refused to complete the work so I ended up suggesting and writing for him. At the end of the lesson I explained that I wanted the four groups to demonstrate (as a TV chef might) how to make a sandwich of their choice. They should bring ingredients.

The second lesson took place next day. I brought ingredients and showed a clip from a TV Cookery programme. Paul had arrived with all the ingredients needed for his group (the only one in the class to bring anything). He watched the video calmly, taking in and using the genre to lead and prepare his own group in an excellent demonstration. He displayed leadership, oral skill, understanding of the subject and the genre, and charm and skill in explanation.

On reflection this incident reminded me of Shirley Brice Heath's work on narrative skills at home and school (1982). She describes three neighbourhoods in the Southeastern region of the U.S. and the different ways that children 'take from printed stories'. She argues that:

"...how mainstream, school oriented children come to learn from books at home suggests that such children learn not only how to take reading from books, but also how to talk about it....they practise (home) routines which parallel those of classroom interaction".

Children from two other communities in the area do not learn these skills in the same way before they come to school and are therefore handicapped in their school careers:

"They do not....observe the rules of linearity in writing, and their expression of themselves on paper is very limited. Orally taped stories are often much better, but these rarely count as much as written composition. Thus Trackton

children continue to collect very low or failing grades, and may decide by the end of sixth grade to stop trying and turn their attention to the heavy peer socialisation which begins in these years".

Paul's attitude to literacy in general tended to reflect this. He was interested in the subject matter of the lesson. He made some attempt to please me and conform to school behaviour by completing the form in writing. He found it difficult, so refused to finish, but was well able to complete the task orally and could not see the point of the writing in between.

Another incident underlines Paul's attitude to the role of literacy in practical tasks. I was setting up the computer in preparation for an email project which I will describe later. He watched me use the printed sheet of instructions for getting into email. It was a different procedure from my computer at home and I was unfamiliar with it. He said, "What do you need that for? You just do it like this". He took over completely and logged on with a password that he was not supposed to know without reference to the printed sheet. He handed back to me when we were ready to email. He was not confident when it came to writing; but he was well able to negotiate his way through life and technology with minimal reading and writing. He did not need the printed props that seem so essential to us in school. He had learned practical procedures that would do just as well.

Another activity which had absorbed and interested Paul had been a task chosen from a number of activities to do with food. The task was as follows:

'Make a booklet in the shape of an egg. Write down 5 things that you can do with an egg. Use a page for each suggestion.'

He completed the task independently; used a dictionary and a recipe book to find words that he needed. He worked quietly and competently to complete the task, cutting and making the different sorts of eggs from yellow and white

He was not confident when it came to writing; but he was well able to negotiate his way through life and technology with minimal reading and writing. He did not need the printed props that seem so essential to us in school.

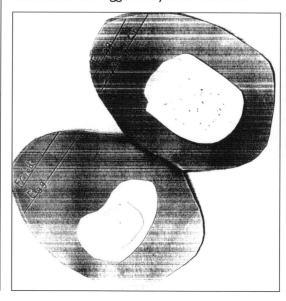

card. On each page he wrote just two words – fried egg, egg sandwich, boiled egg and so on.

He had stripped the task down to its essentials and produced minimal writing. He felt no need to explain in writing how to make a boiled egg, he knew that if necessary he could demonstrate or explain by talking.

Paul responded well to another practical activity based around story. We had been looking at story – plot, character, setting. We had used stories which young children might like to illustrate this. The task was to make a game around a story. Paul's group chose 'The 3 Little Pigs'. When he knew there was little writing involved Paul again took leadership of the group, used a plan (again with minimal writing) worked hard at creating the game, using the computer to create pictures and suggesting ideas for the stop-go cards. I was amazed to see him start to write these out. When I looked again, five minutes later, he had persuaded another more able writer to complete this task. Similarly, during another literacy session, when he was reluctant to come to class at all because he suspected he might have to do some writing, his attitude changed and he joined in with gusto when he found out that his task was actually to create a taped story.

Organising a French Party for a younger class was an activity that caught Paul's attention. He was keen to discuss, plan, and organise equipment. He showed interest in writing invitations and took over this task completely, working collaboratively with another pupil, using a computer package to print invitations and writing all the names himself (from a printed list) by hand. I believe that he cold see a point to this and again it involved minimal writing (although this amounted to quite a lot for him).

A visit to a supermarket to learn about storing, buying and selling food provoked similar interest. Paul completed a letter to the supermarket – finding relevant sentences, placing them in correct order and adding his own message at the bottom. He could do this

> When he knew there was little writing involved Paul again took leadership of the group

easily, he could see a point to it and again it involved practical organisation and minimal writing.

Another means of writing for Paul was through dictation. I was very keen for him to produce some independent writing of his own. It was only in structured lessons, when a group feedback from the trip to the supermarket or the French Party was an element of the lesson, that I allowed dictation, but when Paul was working with another teacher or a Teaching Assistant this might happen. His contribution to group writing was usually full, relevant and although colloquial, he mainly observed the conventions of sequencing and reporting.

His contribution to a group poem called 'The Magic Box' (for which the stimulus was Kit Wright's poem 'The Magic Box') was worthy of note. In this case I do believe that he was caught by the magic of the poem used as a stimulus and wanted to create/write his own poem. He was certainly proud of the poem. You can see the careful illustration that he completed to go with it – even though he persuaded the Teaching Assistant to write for him so that he could write over her writing.

I think that this points to another element in Paul's attitude to writing. He has no confidence in himself as a writer. At the age of thirteen he is big, strong and powerful. He can ride a horse, plant seeds and make them grow, find his way around, use tools competently, argue his case, and so on. But when he looks at his efforts at writing beside those of his mainstream peers, or even others in his class, he knows that they do not compare in quality. He has failed

Dear Sir

We are doing a topic about food.

We would like to come and visit your store to find out about how food is sold.

In our class there are 8 pupils.

Three of the pupils in our class are in wheelchairs.

Two teachers would come with us on our visit

The best time for us to visit would be Tuesday Wednesday or Thursday afternoon.

We could be there at 1.30 p.m.
ples ritbac

yours sincerely

Party Invitation!

Dear Lee
You are invited to a party on:
29.11.00
at: nu?(C.Rom

Party starts at: 2.15 – 300
Love from Year 9.

> ### The Magic Box
>
> By
>
> I would put in my box bay, red and blue.
> The twitch of a rabbit's red nose.
> The neigh of a bay horse.
> The blue of a fishes fin.
>
> I would put in my box
> Dexter, Zorro, Tom and Jerry.
> Tom and Jerry chasing each other.
> Zorro's sword to swish around.
>
> I would put in my box
> 'Get up Martin. It's time for school.
> Your breakfast is ready.
> Hurry up and get dressed'.
>
> I would put in my box
> A sip of Pepsi that would turn you into a bubble.
> A portion of fish that would turn you into a crab.
> A packet of cheese and onion crisps that would turn you into a potato.
>
> My box is made of the bones of a giant. The skin of a leopard.

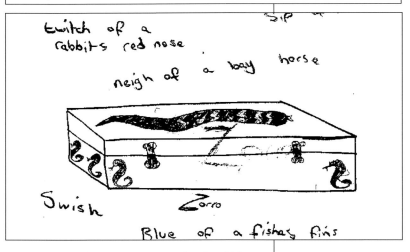

consistently in his own eyes, so why should he bother now?

Would computers help?

Since our school was involved in NOF/ICT Training I had, with my colleague Jennifer Bailey, decided to try an email project with my group of reluctant writers. The idea was to email a Year 6 group within the school. We envisaged emails flying backwards and forwards between the classes – very motivating. They did not exactly fly, but pupils were engaged with the task. Nicholas McGuinn's paper on 'Electronic communication and Under Achieving Boys' in *English in Education* helped me to reflect on the issues. He suggests that:

"….the 'frame' provided by the computer screen has the potential either to offer a supportive structure upon which boys can build – or to become yet another means by which their academic failure can be measured"

In the course of his article he raises:

"….the two issues which are of particular concern to underachieving boys – technical competence and self esteem.'

He points out the advantage of '…encouraging pupils (who find writing slow and painstaking)…. to think of Email writing as though it were a conversation…. (it contains the possibility to) raise their sense of self esteem and focus their attention on the real business of effective communication".

As I was introducing this work to my group of boys, I explained how email was somewhere in between a letter and a telephone conversation. I told them that it was the communication of the future and stressed that in email it did not matter about spelling or punctuation. But at this point Paul reminded me of the mobile phone and that this could do away with writing altogether.

Paul knew emailing was writing and remained suspicious of it at first, handing over to me or others when he could, and sitting back in his chair. I did however sometimes catch him leaning forward and participating in the writing. He enjoyed correcting punctuation, and appreciated the communication element in email. He worked in collaboration with others (which he often found difficult) during this project. But I think that he always saw the potential for 'academic failure' that McGuinn mentions.

McGuinn points out that I.T. can be useful to an English teacher as boys are likely to respond to the technology (anything involving buttons and switches is fun). It can give them a chance to don 'the mantle of the expert', as Paul demonstrated with me when he went into the email package.

Another strand that I investigated with some effect with Paul was humour. My colleague, Angela Bull, took a literacy lesson where she used photographs of her pets and asked pupils to put in speech balloons to indicate what the pets were saying. This really appealed to Paul. He produced eight speech balloons with funny comments in, with hardly a moan about writing.

I managed on another occasion to combine I.T., collaborative work, humour and writing in an activity for my group of reluctant writers. The website ideas.co.uk/english/story.htm provides a frame for a story that was ideally suited to Paul. The idea was to fill in twenty boxes with one word answers and the computer would generate a story from the answers. All four boys in the group enjoyed this. They wrote in a few words like 'bum' which they regarded as hugely funny and were rewarded with a real story at the end of writing just twenty words.

English as a 'feminine area'

I wrote previously of other, more underlying problems which I felt affected Paul's attitude to writing. One of these was the problem of boys' developing masculinity and their perception of

English as being a feminine area. Elaine Millard in her book *Differently Literate*, explores the influence of gender on schooling. She refers to much research which shows that reading and writing are increasingly seen as activities more appropriate to girls than boys. The media and marketing further stress this. She goes on to document the importance to boys of their own sense of their developing masculinity:

"Activities that are seen as girl-preferred are surrounded with far more taboos for boys than boy-preferred activities are for girls. Dressing in male attire, acquiring boys' toys, and trying on a male role is part of most girls' early experience. The role models they encounter reinforce the positive aspects of masculinity…. The female role on the other hand is always an area that acts as trangressive for boys, an area for disquiet or ridicule." (Millard 1997).

It follows that if reading and writing, and English as a whole, are regarded as female pursuits they will be an area to be avoided for boys wishing to establish their masculine identity. This is even more so for boys who attend a Special School.

Paul is fourteen. He is anxious to establish and maintain his masculine identity. He refers in the questionnaire to his mother being the main writer of the family. His father "can't hardly spell" and according to Paul used to "bunk off school". Paul obviously regards him with respect as he runs his own business, without the need for writing. When Paul has time away from school he helps out there.

Paul responds differently to the male staff at school. Male teachers take most of the practical subjects at school which involve no writing. As part of his behaviour programme Paul has a reward on a Friday afternoon of joining an Outdoor Pursuits programme where the male teacher has made a separate agreement with Paul that there will be no writing.

All teachers of English in the school are female. The three male teachers teach PE, Technology, Art, ICT and Maths. Perhaps we need to look at this. More writing linked to practical subjects may be an answer. I really have no hard evidence for this being a factor in Paul's attitude to writing, but I have a gut feeling that this is really important.

What did Paul achieve?

Paul had achieved almost all of the targets set for him at the end of Year 8.

He had written an account of his outdoor activities at school on email – very brief and without punctuation, but still an account. He had also contributed to a dictated group account of a trip to the supermarket and the French Party. He was certainly aware of whether a piece of writing is complete, but only when dictating was he able to complete it himself. He had written a story with a beginning,

a middle and an end – The Giant Egg and produced an exciting taped story. He has contributed to a group poem – The Magic Box. To give him full credit for this work his oral contribution must be taken into account, which I believe it should.

Paul had shown progress in all aspects of English:

Speaking and Listening – He listens well, even when appearing not to. He was able to recall and recount information (amazing his science teacher by recounting which chromosomes made a girl or boy, after watching a video on reproduction). He was able to process information, plan and take a leadership role in group projects (Making a sandwich). He still had some problems with turn taking.

Reading – He now showed much more enjoyment when reading with the group. He sometimes asked to read and when engaged with the reading material would read most words correctly (especially if he could act them). He was able to read set 1/2 NLS high frequency words and spell the first set.

Writing – He was able to compose a story with a beginning, middle and end. He was able to compose an account of an event, a letter and a poem. He was able to spell set 1 of the NLS high frequency words, but did not use these consistently in his writing.

Behaviour – This still fluctuated. There was a measurable link between his bad behaviour and his writing. He approached practical subjects much more readily and would usually participate cooperatively in the part of the lesson that was oral or active.

> …if reading and writing, and English as a whole, are regarded as female pursuits they will be an area to be avoided for boys wishing to establish their masculine identity.

Although he had some periods of exclusion from school, these had decreased during the last year and he was still with us. He had not become a statistic as one of the number of boys excluded.

Some Conclusions

At the start of this project I set out to examine the problems that boys with S.E.N. have with writing and to suggest some ways that will encourage and motivate these boys to write. I listed earlier Paul's problems with writing. I believe that these are problems common to many boys in the bottom streams of secondary schools in this country.

Other problems made evident by my study are:-

- Paul's regular failure to see the relevance of writing to the task in hand.
- The issue of boys' developing masculinity and their perception of English as being a feminine area.
- Issues of self esteem.

Questions which arose during the project:

- *What counts as writing in an S.E.N. context?*

I have argued that we should consider accrediting composition through dictation as writing. This sort of writing can demonstrate planning and structure, as well as capturing ideas in stories and poems. We already accept writing from physically disabled pupils using amanuensis (e.g. examination entries), the more common this practice becomes the more important it seems that we give similar assistance to children like Paul, who find the physical act of writing yet another barrier to composition. Similarly, tape recordings and video could be evidence of achievement in oral work, in drama, discussion and presentations.

- *How can we sustain the interest and application of boys with S.E.N. in writing?*

We are living in the 21st century. Pupils at home have access to a plethora of information, story and sound through TV, video and computer. Like Paul they may have 'remote control attention span'. Motivation, and the sustaining of interest, are key factors. Tasks that involve minimal writing can be used to give boys a sense of success and improve their perception of themselves as writers. Technology is a useful tool – like Paul, many boys are adept at using computers and can sometimes be tempted to write through this medium. Relevance can be a key aspect in boys' writing – there must be a point to a particular writing task (e.g. Paul's invitations to a party). Another approach closely linked to this involves incorporating writing into a practical task, where writing itself is not the main aim (e.g. making a game like Paul's Three Little Pigs game). In all writing activities the level of support is crucial; boys who feel insecure or

> Technology is a useful tool – like Paul, many boys are adept at using computers and can sometimes be tempted to write through this medium.

out of their depth in writing will often use poor behaviour to avoid a task they see as too difficult.

- *Are there some ways in which independent writing can take place?*

I have demonstrated in this project some of the ways in which independent writing can take place. It may be very minimal, as in Paul's addition to the letter to the supermarket. It may be in a collaborative situation, as in the email work. It should of course be encouraged. Pupils still need to be challenged and on rare occasions I have managed to persuade a reluctant writer to write on a subject that has really caught their imagination. The right stimulus is crucial in this. A careful selection of reading material that will appeal to the boys in the class is of great importance.

- *What effect does our cultural view of achievement for men and women have on boys' achievement in writing?*
- *What is it about English and literacy in general that make it uncool?*

These last two questions I have found particularly interesting and I have touched on them briefly in this project. They seem to me to hold much of the reason for the difference in achievement in literacy of boys and girls. They are, however, concerned with attitude, peer group pressure and broader cultural issues. These have had an effect on, but have not formed the major part of this research. To gain substantive evidence there will need to be further investigations targeted more specifically at these areas.

Elizabeth Baker
Woodacre Special School, Thurrock

References

Dahl, Roald (1981) *George's Marvellous Medicine* London, Jonathan Cape

Dahl, Roald (1967) *James and the Giant Peach* London, George Allen & Unwin

Firmin, Peter (1989) *Magic Mash (Jets)* London, A & C Black

Brice Heath, Shirley (1983) *Ways with Words. Language, life, and work in communities and classrooms* Cambridge, Cambridge University Press

McGuinn, Nicholas (2000) 'Electronic Communication and Under-achieving Boys: Some Issues' *English in Education* 34(1) pp 50-57

Millard, Elaine (1997) *Differently Literate – boys, girls, and the schooling of literacy* London, Falmer Press

Wright, Kit (1987) *Cat Among the Pigeons* London, Viking Kestrel
Includes the poem 'The Magic Box'

CHAPTER 6

I don't actually like writing because I can't do it

Victoria Purbrick

How can teachers help boys' be more motivated and interested in writing? In this case study the teacher introduces writing journals as a way of giving boys more choice and control over their writing.

Introduction

The context

I work in a school that has been through a period of rapid change and improvement. However, despite the improvements made so far, all of the staff are fully aware that the standards of writing in our school are below that of national average. Last year's test results showed that 65% of children achieved level 4 or above, which was down 10% on the national average. Of this 65% the majority were girls, which means that as well as looking at how to raise the standards of all the children we specifically need to address the problems encountered by boys.

I wanted to look at the issues boys had with writing in my Year 6 class, but first I reflected on the type of writers I had in my class and found I could divide my class into the following groups:

- Those who can write and will do so readily.
- Those who can write but who will do as little as possible.
- Those who will try anyway and are often pleased with results.
- Those who cannot and don't

Each group contains boys and girls but in differing proportions. For this project I decided to focus on a group of boys in the last three categories.

Issues around motivation

My first question was to look at motivation – why did so many children not want to write.

I decided first to use a writing survey to try to find out more about what the five boys in my study group thought about writing: about their attitude to writing, why they thought we needed to write and what kind of writing they did in and out of school.

> My first question was to look at motivation – why did so many children not want to write.

Their responses to whether they liked writing were mixed:

'No because it is boring for me'.

'Sometimes I like writing, it depends on what I am writing about'.

' I do like writing because it helps my thinking'.

' I like writing because its fun, and in some cases you can write what you want'.

' I like writing a bit, it depends on what ever it is'.

'I don't actually like writing because I can't do it'.

The writing mentioned at school was mainly

handwriting, story writing and poems. The boys who were more positive about writing were also writing at home, saying for example:

'At home at weekends I write all the football teams down I think will win that day. I write my betting slips'.

'Plays because I've read lots of books and plays'

'I do crosswords and poems at home'

Focus on attitude

I wanted to go on to to look at ways of helping boys to become more enthusiastic and interested in writing. On the Boys and Writing project I was particularly interested in hearing Lynda Graham talk about the Croydon Project. She described how teachers had used writing journals in their classes with excellent results. We had already had in school 'Books about Books' (BaBs) in which children are encouraged to write about books in any way they like both at home and at school. The work produced in this book is generated from ideas that children have gained from their reading book or the class or group reader. The children know that BaBs is their book for their ideas.

I decided that I would further develop the use of our BaBs books into writing journals. I wanted the children to use these books for any writing that they wanted to do. The aim was that the children would be more enthusiastic to write about what interested them and not just what was asked of them during literacy and extended writing lessons, and also to perhaps change their attitude towards writing. The book would now contain writing about books and also writing that could be initiated in class or carried out independently at home.

'At home at weekends I write all the football teams down I think will win that day'.

What I wanted to achieve

I hoped that by introducing this book I would gain some insights into the boys' approach to writing and would be able to answer some of the questions that interested me.

- Are boys more enthusiastic when writing about a subject they have chosen?
- What subjects are boys choosing to write about? Can this knowledge be used when planning class activities?
- Would the following encourage the boys to write:
  - thinking of their own ideas to write about
  - being able to carry out a piece of writing that is just for themselves?
  - knowing that their piece of writing will be looked at for its content and not with particular emphasis on punctuation and spelling?
- Would the quality of writing improve through the use of this book?

The writing journal

I introduced the 'new' book to the class and explained why I was introducing it. The class decided that it required a new name, and after discussion it was decided that it was to be called 'Bits 'n' BaBs'. We compiled a list of the types of writing that the children could include as well as writing about books. At the time of writing it consisted of:

Letters
Stories
Biographies
Songs / raps
Recipes

Jokes
Instructions and explanations
Football reports
Newspaper articles
Diaries
Poems
Plays
Interviews

I felt it important to remind the children that there was always going to be an audience to their writing in this book as long as they wanted there to be, however if a child wanted something to remain private then that would also be respected.

Using the writing journal

The structure of the school day means that there is half an hour between the end of play before the start of either maths or literacy, and so one of these sessions per week would be given to ' Bits 'n' BaBs'. The children were also free to take these books home to finish any work or to write about anything that they want to.

One piece of homework each week was going to be the Writing Journal. I used this as an opportunity to introduce a homework contract to confirm that homework, particularly written homework, has to be done. I wanted the children, and especially reluctant boys, to write and more importantly to find things (at home) that they actually wanted to write about. This also coincided with parents' evening and the parents were told of the contract. Everyone was keen to sign the contract, all using fancy signatures that are now permanently on display on the contract.

I used the homework contract to introduce flexible topics for homework, for example, 'choose a newspaper report to give an opinion on, to rewrite or to change the headline'. In this way each child can pick on an article that they find interesting. As a result of the success the homework contract system has been introduced into every classroom and is proving to be just as positive.

Evidence of change

Benefits of the writing journals

All the class have benefited, not just the focus group of boys. Although it must be said that the children who have used it the most have been the ones who have actually not needed it the most! However there are three key areas where it has supported the boys' writing:

- more positive response from the boys in the group
- the improvements in self esteem
- the wider range of writing chosen

I have found the book a good way of getting to know what the children are interested in and also to engage in a dialogue with the writer.

More positive response

There have been a few welcome surprises as a result of the book. One member of the focus group was not really an active member of the classroom environment and did not often volunteer to share his work. This all changed just before Christmas. He had recorded an episode of *Keenan and Kel* and had listened to and written down the lyrics of a song that had been sung in it. To the amusement of the class and to myself he performed it during a class party. The applause at the end was fantastic and everyone was amazed. This child admitted that he probably would not have bothered writing down the song if he did not have this book.

I have found the book a good way of getting to know what the children are interested in and also to engage in an informal dialogue between yourself and the writer. It also provides a permanent place for work that previously may have been done on a scrap piece of paper and never shared with anyone.

Self Esteem

Another child's self-esteem in writing was a problem. M is a child who constantly measures his ability in terms of how other children (particularly boys) are doing. If he realises that most of the other children are ahead of him, he panics, then cries and shuts off instead of trying to catch up with the rest. Homework was also a problem but with the combination of the homework contract and the introduction of the book he now makes a much better effort and is much more confident in sharing his work with a small audience.

The Types of Writing Chosen

The journals gave the boys in the group the freedom to follow their own interests in writing and I was interested to note a more varied picture of writing preferences and stimuli for writing emerging. Writing in the journals included:

- a film adapted and rewritten as a story containing slightly altered characters.
- spin-offs from watching television such as song lyrics from *Keenan and Kel* and *The Fresh Prince of Bel Air.*
- story topics influenced by adventure films and I was struck throughout how much the boys were using visual stimuli for their writing
- the boys in the group have written about sport, of one sort or another. Wrestling on television seems to be the 'thing' of the moment, and for the lower ability boys in the group, seems to be the main influence.
- writing linked to the news when the boys have selected an article either by content, by the headline or by the accompanying photograph.
- topics of interest, so, for example, one boy in the focus group selected volcanoes because

them from books that he had read. He likes to write poems and non-fiction (he has just finished a project on space). He likes to use non-fiction texts to find information because 'the spellings are already there' but he also added that you couldn't just copy, as then 'you are not thinking for yourself'. At home he writes notes to mum and uses the writing journal usually to write poems, although he was aware that his spelling continued to be a deterrent to writing.

Within the group as a whole there does seem to have been a change in attitude and the boys in the group can be heard talking about what they can do in their 'Bits'n'BaBs' book.

In September H stated handwriting as the only writing he did. Now he listed poems, stories, arguments (which he particularly liked doing), posters, experiments, tables and charts and questions and answers. At home he used his B&B book to write down lyrics from television shows and has performed these to the rest of the class; he admitted he would not have done this if he didn't have his B&B book. He has also written match reports and said he now thinks that writing is important to show 'how intelligent you are and to communicate especially through letters'.

E said that he does enjoy writing especially nonsense poetry. He enjoys writing stories because 'with imagination you can do anything that you want'. At home E uses his B&B book for stories and apparently for notes about things he should remember that he has learned in school! At the moment he is writing his autobiography. He thinks that the journal is a good idea as children can write what they want and when they want. When asked what puts him off writing he said ' I wish that you could just say something and it would already be written down'. Thinking about getting his spelling correct used to be a problem but now he knows that that can be improved when redrafting.

At home, P uses his B&B book to write about wrestling, and history especially World War 2. He has written up a science experiment that he has done at home and has also rewritten a Biff and Chip play using friends in the key roles. After using the journal he said that if you cannot write then you are missing out on something good that you can do. As a final comment . said that he needs peace and quiet to write; he cannot concentrate when there is a lot of noise around him. He worries that his work will not be good enough but knows he can reword what he wants to say if he cannot spell something, however this does not matter in his 'Bits'n'BaBs' book.

C still does not do much writing at home but knows that he can write about personal things and does not have to worry about handwriting and spelling.

he assumed (and quite rightly) that there would be a lot of animations on the Internet as well as wonderfully coloured books for him to use. Space was another topic chosen for this reason.

A Change in Attitude

After using the journals for a couple of months I decided to ask the group again about their attitudes to see if there had been any positive changes since September and was pleased that the group does seem to be more aware of what is expected of them in writing (but luckily this does not seem to be intimidating them). This is obviously due to a number of reasons including the project that the school is doing in order to raise standards in writing. The boys are becoming more aware that a good piece of writing is a lot more than just correct spellings and neat handwriting.

The biggest change came from M. At the beginning of Year 6 his self-esteem in writing was very low, he constantly rubbed out his work so very little writing was actually done. If homework involved writing he rarely did it. In September he fitted the category ' can't write, doesn't write', he also thought that writing was 'boring'. This time he was clear that writing was no longer boring. He said that spelling had been the major factor putting him off writing but now ideas came more easily as he knew he could get

He enjoys writing stories because 'with imagination you can do anything that you want'.

Reflecting on the project

For me personally it has been quite a surprise to discover the extent to which the focus group have been put off in the past by the need to get spellings correct and by the expectation to get handwriting as neat as possible. Although there is no getting away from the fact that these are important requirements, I feel that I should also remember that there is a lot more to a piece of writing than just these aspects. As a result the thought process and the planning of a structured piece of work will be a focus from now on in my class.

In future I will make more explicit my expectations for spelling, for example that the more familiar words are to be spelled correctly and attempts at new words are to be underlined by the child as they write. As for handwriting, I will continue to encourage those who are slow and untidy to use their extra handwriting book at home as well as the practice they do at school, the aim being to speed up their writing so that it is not hindering the thought process.

Changing Attitude, Increasing Enthusiasm

I feel that the book has helped to make all the children a little more enthusiastic about writing. It has certainly helped to change the attitude of the least motivated children who now are often writing because they want to, rather than because they have been told to.

The quality of writing has not really improved as a result of this book, only the quantity has. I do not feel too despondent about this as I feel that building the children's confidence with their writing is very important and improving quality can come next, although by the middle of Year 6 I have to accept that only small improvements will now be made. I think the writing journal has the potential to be used from a younger age to encourage a good attitude towards writing from the start.

Room for Improvement

The journal was intended to be used at school and at home, yet at the end of the project I feel that nearly all the writing in it has been done at home. I plan to continue with this book and to plan to use it more during Literacy lessons.

One area that did not work was the 'personal' aspect of the book. We soon discovered that its secrecy could not be guarded due to the nature of the sharing aspect – which often included reading other people's work not just listening to it, so secrets or problems that the children wanted to write down couldn't be guaranteed to remain private.

When focusing on a new 'project' whatever that may be, other things are often left to drop, usually unintentionally. This happened in our

class with the 'BaBs' aspect of the book and writing about books came second to other types of writing in it. So many rewarding activities, stimulated by almost any book, can be carried out in BaBs and in the words of J, they can provide help in showing him and lots of other children how to write.

Victoria Purbrick
Abbots Hall Junior School, Thurrock

A secondary English teacher examines the gap between boys' and girls' attainment and, through action research, seeks to understand more about the roots of difference, about girls' and boys' attitudes to literacy, and about what can affect these attitudes. She finds the role of the teacher to be crucial in effecting change.

Differently literate, or literally different?

Emma Scott-Stevens

Aims

My aims in this project were:
- To use action research to understand the relationship between boys' attitudes to writing and their attainment in English.

- To use this understanding to change and improve understanding and practice, and to raise the attainment of boys in English.

The reasons for my research

There were two main reasons for my interest in the area of boys and writing.

1 The first reason was GCSE results. The GCSE results for English in my school for both boys and girls are close to the national average (girls slightly above, boys slightly below) as shown in the table below. However, even though this is the case, there is still a *significant difference* in attainment between girls and boys. This was one of the main reasons for my involvement in this project.

Year 2000 GCSE English A* - C grades		
	Girls	Boys
National Average	66%	51%
My School	68%	49%

As the statistics show 19% more girls than boys achieve a C or above in their English GCSE.

2 This gap between boys and girls was also reflected in the qualitative feedback from teachers in the English department regarding the achievement of boys. In addition to the gap shown by the statistics it was also felt that boys were more likely

> In addition to the gap shown by the statistics it was also felt that boys were more likely to fall behind with coursework, and once having done this struggled to catch up.

to fall behind with coursework, and once having done this struggled to catch up. This often led to them losing motivation before the course was completed. It was felt that this was not only contributing to their lack of success at GCSE, but also creating behaviour problems in the classrooms.

Action research

For my action research I completed two projects: firstly, a small project with 6 'low achieving' boys in Year 10; and secondly, a questionnaire with pupils from the top and bottom groupings exploring their attitudes to writing.

Small group work

This project involved:

- Discussion with Key Skills Year 10 group – 13 boys, 2 girls from which the smaller sample was selected.
- A questionnaire used before and after small group work to record general attitudes.
- 6 pupils involved in the small group work (over a two month period).
- Writing an essay discussing poetry – evidence of pupils' writing before the project and an essay produced at the end.
- Informal discussions with pupils before, during and after small group work.

Findings

All pupils involved improved the quality of their work and their GCSE grade (see fig i)

Discussions with the pupils involved found that the following factors can have a positive influence on the motivation of boys to write:

- sense and awareness of the purpose of writing;
- collaborative support from peers in a small group setting;
- enthusiasm and interest of the teacher.

However, the questionnaire responses reveal that although in the small group environment pupils were willing to change their attitude, long term change of their overall attitude to writing was difficult to sustain in the secondary school classroom. In the normal classroom environment pupils were still often negative about writing tasks.

Pupil 1

Baseline information – taken from 'Of Mice and Men' coursework

Reading
- shows some understanding of character;
- shows some understanding of cultural context through comments on Crooks.

Writing
- organised competently – uses sentences and paragraphs;
- handwriting legible most of the time;
- spelling accurate for common words;
- some awareness of audience of this writing, although several uses of non standard English.

Additional Comments – GCSE grade F

This pupil shows clear understanding of the characters in the novel studied, but does not show any understanding of the essay form. There is some evidence of lack of effort here. The pupil's work does show some inappropriate use of language with the use of non-standard English. The work shows no reference to the text.

Work produced after small group work

Reading
- makes response to text, makes connections between the texts;
- shows understanding of context and setting;
- makes reference to the text when exploring views.

Writing
- makes connections and comparisons between texts in his writing
- organised competently – uses sentences and paragraphs, although some sentence boundaries missing;
- handwriting legible most of the time;
- spelling accurate for common words;
- some awareness of audience, although several uses of non standard English.

Additional Comments – GCSE grade E

This pupil shows clear understanding of the poems studied and conveys this in a structured essay form, although there is still some non-standard usage. The work shows reference to the texts studied. Effort is still an issue here, although with further work this pupil's GCSE grade could be improved further.

Fig I

1 Please place the following writing activities in the boxes below.

- answering questions
- brainstorming
- writing a factual report
- making notes from a written text
- writing a story
- filling in the missing words in a piece of text
- writing a poem
- planning activities
- writing a newspaper article
- writing an essay.

I enjoy this	I don't mind this	I don't like doing this

2 How would you describe your attitude to writing? (please circle one)

I enjoy all writing activities.   I don't enjoy writing most of the time

I enjoy some writing activities   I never enjoy writing

3. Why do you enjoy/not enjoy writing? (please be as detailed as possible)

. . . .

. . . .

4

Would any of the following factors influence you to improve your writing?

(please tick)

	Would definitely improve it	Might improve it	Would make no difference
Competing with my friends to be the best at writing			
An enthusiastic teacher who is interested in me			
Targets that have been set by a teacher			
Targets that I have set Myself			
My parents encouraging me And helping me with my work			

5   Read the following statements carefully. **Circle** the words that best describe your opinion.

i)   **Girls work harder than boys**

         True   True most of the time   True some of the time   Not true

ii)   **Boys don't behave as well as girls**

         True   True most of the time   True some of the time   Not true

iii)   **Boys don't bother as much about school work as girls**

         True   True most of the time   True some of the time   Not true

iv)   **Girls care more about learning than girls**

         True   True most of the time   True some of the time   Not true

v)   **Boys are given more attention in class than girls**

         True   True most of the time   True some of the time   Not true

Questionnaire

This project involved:

- Further research to consider how pupils' attitudes to writing develop throughout KS3. How do pupils reach the position where they feel unable to be successful writers?

- A questionnaire (see appendix 2) that was used to provide more quantitative data across KS3 regarding boys' attitudes.

- A sample size of 30 (5 pupils were selected from the highest and lowest groupings in Years 7, 8 and 9).

Findings

- Interestingly, writing stories was named as a writing activity that 25 out of the 30 pupils in the sample enjoyed (83%).

- 15 of the pupils involved named writing essays as an activity that they don't enjoy doing (50%).

- The main reasons for enjoying writing were:

  – writing being fun

  – using their imagination

  – expressing themselves.

- The main reason for not enjoying writing was because it was seen as boring.

- Teachers were seen as the most important influence upon writers. 14 pupils (46%) stated that 'an enthusiastic teacher who is interested in me' would definitely help them to improve their writing. In addition to this 13 pupils (43%) stated that this might help them to improve, with only 2 pupils (6%) stating that this would make no difference.

- Parents and peers were also seen as important influences.

- An interesting contrast arose when comparing the data from the high sets and low sets. When comparing the high sets the number of pupils who stated certain influences 'would definitely' improve their writing remained constant over Years 7, 8 and 9. However, the data from the lowest sets showed a marked decline in the number of pupils who believed that others could influence their writing. This may reflect the feelings of boys who lose motivation to write and reinforce their failure, therefore believing that there is less chance that their writing can be improved.

- In response to a number of statements about gender, pupils were asked to state to what extent the statements were true. I expected clear stereotypes to emerge, but

40

this did not really happen. There was a mix of responses; around 50% of the sample agreeing that some of the statements were true at least some of the time. There was only a slight difference between the high and low ability pupils, with the low ability pupils more likely to agree with the stereotypical statements.

Conclusions

- Most importantly, the role of the teacher is crucial to raising the attainment of boys' (and all pupils') writing. This was reflected in both the small group work and the results of the questionnaires.

- Collaborative support from peers is also important and can improve writing when in a positive environment.

- More emphasis needs to be placed upon purpose when teaching and modelling writing. Interestingly, the questionnaire reflected boys enjoying story writing rather than favouring non-fiction, as is often stereotypically assumed. It may be, however, that when boys do favour non-fiction writing it is because they clearly understand how to do it, its purpose and audience.

- Attitudes to writing can be changed and this can improve pupils' achievement in writing. For this to be sustained, a whole school approach to teaching writing would be beneficial to reflect and improve upon the successes of small group work such as mine.

Overall my action research has helped me to consider closely the relationship between boys and writing. It has raised many questions that myself and my department are going to explore further as we develop our practice.

Emma Scott-Stevens
Gable Hall School, Thurrock

These success stories from Croydon classrooms show teachers engaged in action research about teaching writing. Changes in teachers' practice brought about changes in boys' & girls' competence in writing. An important feature in successful classrooms was teachers' readiness to help children create imaginary worlds through writing.

Teachers as experts in learning

Lynda Graham

'The most important things about writing are spelling and handwriting'. Mark, age 7, was talking to his teacher, Tracey Newvell. She was surprised to find that the transcriptional features of writing were of such over-riding importance to Mark, and began to interview other children in her Y2 class. They too shared Mark's perception about the paramount importance of spelling and handwriting. Tracey began to wonder about the messages she herself was giving to children in her teaching of writing. These interviews took place at the beginning of Tracey's involvement in the Croydon Writing Project, and it may be helpful at this stage to give a brief outline of the project itself.

The Project

The Project aims to provide a supportive structure that will enable busy classroom teachers to engage in thoughtful action research about the teaching of writing. With this support, teachers work to discover new ways of teaching writing that will raise standards. A similar project design had been supportive to teachers engaged in research about the teaching of reading (Graham 1999). Tracey's research took place in the second year of the four-year Croydon Writing Project. In the first year teachers had made significant discoveries about the teaching of writing, particularly in relation to boys (Graham 2001). Tracey and her fellow teacher researchers aimed to build on these discoveries as they engaged in action research in their own classrooms.

Action research model

Our research follows an action research model, in which three sources of evidence are central to the research: interview, observation and documentation. Teachers have conversations

with the children and listen intently to what they have to say. They observe children carefully as they write, and study pieces of writing. Their aim in all this is to be more effective teachers. Garth Boomer claimed: *'All teachers should be experts in 'action research' so that they can show all students how to be 'action researchers'. That is, all teachers should be experts in learning so that they can remind all students how to learn'* (Boomer 1985).

Our research follows an action research model, in which three sources of evidence are central to the research: interview, observation and documentation.

Inset Programme

Teachers are supported in their research by a two-term programme of Inset. They meet with me on a regular basis to share their research findings. For instance, Tracey shared her despair that so many children seemed to be focusing on transcriptional aspects of writing. In discussion she was reassured to hear that other teachers had experienced similar problems. Later in the project, the group shared her excitement and renewed interest in teaching as she began to introduce new ways of teaching writing. Other teachers began to take on some of Tracey's ideas, and she in turn developed ideas taken from colleagues. Bruner realised that '…*most learning in most settings is a communal activity, a sharing of the culture*' (Bruner1986). This is true for Writing Project teachers; each group becomes a powerful community of teacher researchers.

In this sharing session, teachers also develop their thinking through writing. As this is a project about writing, so we ourselves need to experience the writing process (Graves 1983), using writing as a tool for thinking. Teachers write reflectively to me and I reply in writing, giving encouragement and highlighting aspects of their research that feel interesting. This writing is informal, a talking aloud on paper. I have adapted the useful reading response framework devised by Chambers (1993) and now invite teachers to think about things that have surprised and puzzled them in their research, and about questions they are asking.

The second half of each Inset session is designed for teachers to hear experienced researchers talk about the teaching of writing. When I worked as a co-ordinator for the National Oracy Project it was a great joy for me to listen to and work with people who had themselves undertaken research in speaking and listening. I wanted Project teachers to have similar opportunities. During the first year of the Writing Project we invited Myra Barrs and Val Cork to talk about the CLPE research into Literature and Writing (Barrs & Cork 2001), a session which not only shaped the thinking of current Project teachers but also influenced the project design. A central feature of the project is now a drama workshop, giving teachers the confidence to use drama to explore texts actively with children, and help them to use these understandings in their own writing.

As part of the Inset series, teachers from previous modules share their research. Annette Johnson told the story of her discoveries about Writing Journals (Johnson 2000), and some teachers in the group took ideas from this into their own research. Heidi McClusky's discovery of the importance of children hearing directly about the writing process from a published writer (McClusky 1999) shaped the design of the project itself. Author workshops are now a central feature of the Project.

Case study design

Project teachers work on changes to teaching with all children in the class. But they monitor the effect of these changes by studying two children in depth; these are their case study children. These pupils are chosen carefully. Teachers first assess the class using the

> A central feature of the project is now a drama workshop, giving teachers the confidence to use drama to explore texts actively with children, and help them to use these understandings in their own writing.

appropriate CLPE writing scale (CLPE 1997). In addition, they identify the ethnicity of each child in the class and assess the median for black, Asian and white boys and girls in the class to see whether there are significant areas of underachievement. Using all this information, they then choose their two children; usually one girl and one boy are chosen. It is important that case study children are representative of significant groups of children in the class, as successful changes to teaching will then impact on the greatest number of children in the class.

Assessment of progress

At the end of each module each teacher re-assesses the class, and then calculates the percentage of children who have moved on at least one level on the writing scale. In order to examine trends across the project, we calculate the overall percentage movement. In the first year we were delighted to find that 72% of children had moved on at least one level on the Writing Scale, and that of these children 73% were girls and 71% boys. This indicated that changes to teaching were effective for both girls and boys. This was significant as in our LEA, at the beginning of the project, the gap between the achievement of boys and girls in writing was one of the largest in the country.

However, at the end of the first year of the project I also analysed the accumulated data in terms of ethnicity, and found that the lowest achieving group were black boys (only 63% had moved on at least one level). It seemed we needed to be more pro-active in relation to this group in the second year of the project. In Tracey's year all teachers once again identified the modal average for boys and for girls. Then, if there was a black boy within this level he was chosen as the case study boy.

The stories in the section that follows give some glimpses into the accumulated evidence which was the bedrock of the teachers' action research.

Autonomy in teaching

The project contains many stories of teachers determined to find ways of involving all children in the writing communities they create. They are stories of children becoming writers, but they are also stories of teachers' re-discovered joy in teaching.

Teachers in the Project are given autonomy to make changes to their teaching of writing. In the process, they take risks, explore new ways of teaching and develop their own considered philosophies about the teaching of writing. (Medwell 1998) Some have been in teaching for only a couple of years, others for more than thirty. All make very real changes to their teaching and a difference to the lives of their children as writers.

The case studies that follow are of four boy writers in the second year of the Writing Project. They are chosen from those classes in which the greatest percentage of both boys and girls made progress in their writing. Like many other boys, at the beginning of the research these boys did not choose to write, and looked on writing in school as a necessary chore. Their stories are examples of the creative and insightful ways in which project teachers changed the teaching of writing to enable all children, including reluctant boy writers, to make significant progress as writers.

Reception class: Greg

Carol Domingo, an experienced Reception teacher and Language Co-ordinator, studied Greg, a white boy born in the UK. Her school serves a largely middle class area. End of key stage test results are higher than average, but despite this the achievement of boys in writing was lower than for girls. Carol was concerned as her observations across the school led her to realise that most boys did not write from choice. She wondered whether children's experience of writing in the Reception year contributed to this disenchantment.
Her case study boy, Greg, did not choose to write. (All children's names are pseudonyms.)

In her early observations, Carol noticed that, given the choice, Greg played on the floor away from adults in the classroom, or played outside. This was similar for most boys in the class. In contrast, girls were drawn to the writing corner and to working at tables sitting alongside adults. Already, at the beginning of life in school, girls were choosing to write but boys were not.

Carol was confident that Greg would make progress in writing. She is an experienced teacher of literacy. Her programme includes singing and chanting poems and rhymes, reading stories aloud, shared writing, introducing children to the world of print, and inviting children to use the tunes of repetitive texts to create their own. She knew that, with these experiences, most children did make progress in writing. However, she was concerned that boys were not choosing to write and wondered why. She decided that this would be the focus of her research. How could she engage boys as writers from the very beginning of school?

Mark-making in imaginative play

Carol determined that, as boys were not choosing to write, she would bring writing into the activities they chose. Her early attempts were successful with many boys, but not with Greg. For instance, noticing that a group was having trouble sharing turns with the bikes, she suggested the boys keep a tally. Most accepted this suggestion, not Greg. On another occasion, Carol noticed him playing with a friend on the floor with small play zoo animals. She encouraged the boys to make signs for their zoo with lollipop sticks and small pieces of card. When Carol returned they had indeed made marks on pieces of card. They were willing to interpret these marks, one read: *'The chameleon is giving the elephant a big thump'.* It was clear that the boys had engaged in imaginative play, but Carol had no idea whether or not the labels had been made simply to please her. She decided that in order to find out she needed to work alongside children using mark-making in their play.

Carol initiated the making of a zoo and a model of Lego Land. Encouraged by her, children wrote labels, which included warnings, information, maps, menus and greetings. Many children, including boys, enjoyed making these signs and labels and later incorporated the idea

> Carol determined that, as boys were not choosing to write, she would bring writing into the activities they chose.

of label writing in their own play. For instance, having used all the large bricks to create a fire station, one group of boys set about making their own signs, one of which read, *'Keep out – you might get run over'*. However, Greg took no part in any of these writing activities. He played alongside other children as they wrote labels, but made no attempt himself to make marks.

Writing about what matters to the writer

At the beginning of each week Carol sat with children in a circle on the floor, and encouraged them to talk about what had happened at the weekend. She listened intently and talked with them about their families, television programmes and toys that were important. In his longitudinal study Wells (1986) described how Rosie, full of talk at home, was unable to communicate at school. It was quite different in Carol's classroom. Through careful listening and the interest she showed, Carol enabled children to talk about their worlds together.

One morning Greg arrived at school clutching a new toy dinosaur, and proudly talked about it in his group. After discussion children were invited to draw and then write about their news. Greg's previous writing attempts in class had been faint, timid marks. This time he drew a series of firm letter-like shapes and told Carol he wanted these marks to say, *'I've been sick and I went to the shops and bought a dinosaur, a raptor'*. She scribed his words. This was the first time that Greg had made marks confidently. He had been able to rehearse his writing through talking to others who were interested in what he had to say. He was a knowledgeable dinosaur owner and delighted in bringing his own world into the classroom.

Writing about imagined worlds

Carol thought about Greg's passion for dinosaurs. This was an interest shared by many

> This was the first time that Greg had made marks confidently. He had been able to rehearse his writing through talking to others who were interested in what he had to say.

> Our school improvement project reflects the need to improve boys' performance right across the curriculum.

other children, so she decided to build a Dinosaur Den in the classroom. Children were invited to enter the Den on an imaginary time-machine, and then report back as scientists on their observations. Clip boards and magnifying glasses were provided. Greg was desperate to be chosen and spent a long time in the Den. He emerged with a careful pencil drawing of a pterodactyl. He asked Carol to scribe and dictated: *'A pterodactyl flies. It's got claws on its wings. It's got bumps on its head. It eats fish. It flies through the water and goes underneath the water and grabs them'*. The Dinosaur Den enabled Greg to bring his real expertise into the classroom.

Building on this interest, Carol read aloud *Long Neck and Thunderfoot* (Piers 1982) and invited groups of children to re-enact the story with the small play dinosaurs. Children used the dinosaur props as they created their own story and once again Carol was the scribe. Greg said that the Brontosaurus would *'Body slam them with their tails…Run away and think up a cunning plot…get a net and climb a tree and throw it over the baddies when they were underneath'*. In her study of children's story-telling at home Fox invited children to tape-record the stories they created. (Fox 1993). The tapes captured the children's powerful oral narratives. Greg too was emerging as a storyteller.

Choosing to write

The focus on dinosaurs kindled Greg's interest in writing, and he began to choose to write. He worked with other children and decided with them to change the Dinosaur Den into Jurassic Park. Tickets and price labels were written. Children chose where to write; some wrote lying on the floor or standing with clipboards. Children, including Greg, wrote with enthusiasm because they could write about what mattered to them in real and imagined worlds. In bringing their own popular culture

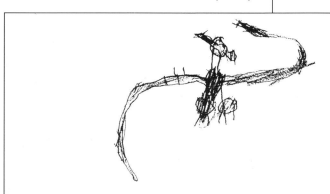

Pterodactyl

A pterodactyl flies. It's got claws on its wings. It's got bumps on its head.

It eats fish. It flies through the water and goes underneath the water and grabs them.

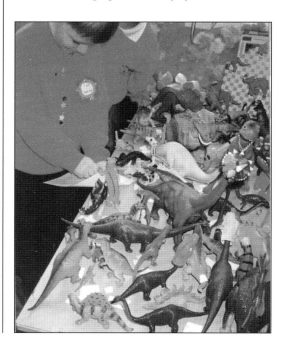

into the classroom, they made links between the worlds of home and school. Marsh and Millard (2000) write about the unifying effect of sharing popular culture like this in the classroom. All children in Greg's class were keen to be part of this classroom community, which was a community in which boys, too, were writers.

Conclusion

In two terms Greg did make expected progress in the skills of writing. At the beginning of school his early marks were faint letter-like shapes. By the end of two terms, with Carol sitting beside him helping him to hear sounds in the words he wanted to say, he wrote: 'I am g to go to cls hs' (I am going to go to Claire's house). In addition, Greg was now choosing to write. For example, at the end of the Project he was playing with friends in an imaginative game with play people. Carol noticed that at home time Greg wrote a notice for the unfinished game. It read: 'anyone who touches the people will get killed'. Greg was beginning to be a writer.

Carol persevered in her research. Early attempts at involving Greg in label making in imaginative play had worked for many children including most boys, but not Greg. She observed him carefully, and began to realise that he really was a story maker and needed to be able to tell the stories that were in his head as he engaged in imaginative play. She supported this story making through scribing for him. Her research enabled all children in the class, including boys, to write about what really mattered to them in a community of fellow writers.

Year 2: Mark

Tracey Newvell was in her tenth year of teaching, and had recently been made Language Co-ordinator in her Infant School. The school is in an area of poverty. A significant number of children are entitled to free school meals and a high percentage of children have English as an additional language. For her case study Tracey chose Mark, a black Caribbean-background boy born in the UK. She was concerned because a *'look of pain'* crossed his face whenever he was asked to write. When asked to give his own assessment of a recently written story, he concentrated solely on technical aspects of the writing: *'It's good because the writing is small, and I've got 66s and 99s'.* This assessment differed markedly from that of Tracey, who was delighted with Mark's lively re-making of the traditional Three Little Pigs story into a story about three little dinosaurs and *'The Big Bad Dino'.*

In talking further with Mark, Tracey was intrigued to find that at home he wrote letters and emails to friends and family, and that he enjoyed this kind of writing. She wondered how

> She observed him carefully, and began to realise that he really was a story maker and needed to be able to tell the stories that were in his head as he engaged in imaginative play.

she could change her teaching so children would begin to experience enthusiasm for writing in the classroom.

Reading aloud for fun

In the first Inset session of the project, Andrew Lambirth (Lambirth 1997) read poems aloud with joy and verve. His input led Tracey to realise that she had barely found time to read aloud to the children for fun. She decided to make time to share her own pleasure in reading aloud to children. Poems were read, re-read, chanted and enjoyed. Children loved humorous poems. Poems from the Caribbean (Agard & Nichols 1996) were shared and children, including Mark, chose to perform them and have a go at talking 'just like mum'. Some poems, like 'Down behind the dustbin' (Rosen 1996) were learnt by heart 'just because we liked them'. Tracey re-discovered her own pleasure in reading aloud, and the children became avid listeners and chanters of poetry. She wondered how she could she kindle this same feeling of joy in writing.

Fun in the Literacy Hour

Tracey decided to bring more fun into the Literacy Hour. She herself had experienced real pleasure in writing in role at a drama workshop led by Teresa Grainger (Grainger and Cremin 2001). She thought hard about how she could bring writing in role into her next unit of work, on speech marks. The text she chose was *This is the Bear* (Hayes 1986). She read the story aloud several times, the children joining in as they became familiar with the text. Next she invited children to work in small groups making physical pictures of sections of the story. These pictures were then 'freeze framed' as she took imaginary photos of the action. From children's movements, and what they said in the freeze frame, it became evident that they were beginning to walk in the shoes of characters from the story.

Would Tracey be able to extend children's involvement in the drama activity to a writing task that would involve a focus on speech marks? She decided to take on two further strategies that had been found to be successful in the first year of our Writing Project: rehearsing thinking through drawing and through talk. She invited children first to draw the characters from their freeze frame. Children had experienced the character through drama; they were now given the opportunity to transform this thinking through another dimension, that of drawing. Tracey invited children to create a picture story text. Having drawn the central characters, children were asked to make speech bubbles, and write what the characters were thinking or saying.

The children drew and wrote with verve. They were experts, having heard and chanted the original text, and experienced the story themselves through drama. They knew the characters well, and wrote powerfully in role in the speech bubbles. When it came to writing the story, the words from the speech bubbles were simply lifted and woven into the narrative. Speech marks replaced bubbles.

Tracey invited children to choose where to sit and to talk about their work in progress. Boys chose to work with boys, and girls with girls. This was to be true whenever children were invited to choose. We first began to realise that gender groupings were important to children in the KS2 Reading Project (Graham 1999) and Writing Project teachers were now finding that gender groupings are equally important for young writers.

Children produced individual pieces of work, and shared their on-going work with each other. They worked in companionship, giving reassurance and praise, and sharing ideas and expertise. It became evident to Tracey that there was a buzz and hum about the work in progress. Children were enjoying the task and were beginning to experience pleasure in being part of a community of writers in the classroom. Earlier, children had delighted in sharing humorous poems. Now this humour and liveliness surfaced in their own writing. For instance, in Mark's picture and narrative the boy says, 'Sit you bad dog you broke my boots and your in bad trouble! Now get on with your work man!'

Becoming a storyteller

Children were having fun in their writing, and Tracey herself was experiencing real joy in teaching. The drama workshop inspired her not only to engage children in drama activities, but

also to make stories. She became a storyteller. The first story she invented was about a spacecraft landing in the school playground. She took a photo and used digital technology to

> They worked in companionship, giving reassurance and praise, and sharing ideas and expertise. It became evident to Tracey that there was a buzz and hum about the work in progress.

make it seem as though a spaceship had landed in the empty playground. Using this picture she told the children what she had seen the previous evening, and then invited them to question her. They bombarded her with questions, and went on to write powerful news reports about the alien landing.

A second invented story was about a boy called Jack who could sleep only if 'he had his tiny bear Russell in his hand'. She showed the children a tiny bear in her own hand. In the story she told children that 'One night he had a terrible dream. He dreamt that something horrible had happened' She then asked them to turn to their partners and say what that terrible thing might be. While they did this she slipped the bear into her pocket, so that she could dramatically show an empty hand when she continued her story. 'When he woke up he breathed a sigh of relief until he noticed something awful. He opened his hand and saw that Russell was **gone!**' Children were completely involved in the story. They too were storytellers. They had imagined what the terrible thing might be. Now they were now invited to work with each other in creating freeze frames as they worked through Jack's quest to find Russell. Later, again working in companionship with each other in gender groups of their own choosing, children went on to write powerful stories about Jack's quest to find Russell.

Finally, Tracey told one last invented story, this time of an imagined walk she had taken in the nearby woods and her discovery of a huge nest with very large eggs. She told the children that the nest appeared to have been abandoned and that she had decided to bring it home. She then produced a large box containing the 'nest'. Gradually it became clear to the spellbound children that the eggs had hatched, and were in fact tiny dinosaurs. Children had previously worked on rhymes with choruses, and Tracey suggested they create a class poem in this style to welcome the dinosaurs to the classroom. Next they were asked to choose a friend to make their own joint poem. All boys chose boys and girls chose girls. The classroom became a noisy hub as children chanted the poems they were creating. They then volunteered to read these poems aloud, and did so with energy. They chose to perform their poems.

Writing Journals

Towards the end of her research Tracey decided to introduce Writing Journals to the class. The idea of Writing Journals had developed in the first year of the Croydon Writing Project (Graham 2001). In these Journals children were given the opportunity to choose what to write. Some teachers entered into a written dialogue with their pupils and others invited children to share entries with one other by reading aloud. Common features were that children could choose what to write, and that teacher and children gave Writing Journals status in the classroom. Mark loved the idea of being able to choose what to write, and in his first entry took the opportunity to ask Tracey if he could *'be in orange group'*. Tracey answered his query, and Mark went on to write enthusiastically about friendships, and about his current passion for Pokemon .

Conclusion

Tracey herself was having fun in her teaching of writing, and this was reflected in children's increased enjoyment and confidence. Interviewed at the end of the research period, Mark stated that he was *'the best writer in the class because I can help other people'*. He had chosen a less experienced writer to be his partner for the work on the dinosaur poem, and this had given him confidence. He felt now that *'humour'* was the most important thing about writing, not spelling and handwriting. He was making expected progress in the transcriptional aspects of writing, but these concerns no longer dominated his thinking. Tracey enabled all children in the class, including boys, to make significant progress as writers. Overall, 89% of the class, including Mark, moved on at least one level on the CLPE Writing Scale. In addition, children were now writing with enjoyment, and were choosing to write. Children were becoming writers.

Year 3: Anthony

Ann Hudson was in her third year of teaching. Her school is an inner city school, with a significant number of children with English as a second language. Ann chose to study Anthony, a black Caribbean-background boy born in the UK. Anthony's initial perceptions of himself as a writer worried Ann. In a written questionnaire Anthony wrote: *'I don't feel like writing now. I don't like writing because it makes me sad because I can't writing well'*.

The Writing Zone

Ann thought hard about ways in which she could encourage Anthony to begin to write without fear. She knew that children in her class loved listening to stories, and sharing, discussing and reading favourite books. How could writing be made to feel just as exciting? She decided to convert a corner of her classroom into a Writing Zone. The term was familiar to the children, as they had recently visited The Dome in London. Children were intrigued as a small, tempting, cave-like structure began to emerge. The headteacher was invited to conduct a grand opening ceremony, and children vied with each other to be chosen to write in the Zone.

Anthony was one of the first children, and loved the choices of stationery, and the freedom to choose what to write. On his first visit he chose

to write about his feelings of being in the Writing Zone itself. In contrast to the feelings of sadness he had expressed in his initial writing interview, this time he focussed on feelings of happiness at being one of the Zone's first visitors. *'When I first came in the Writing Zone I felt great. The zone will surprise you. One day you will come in. The Writing Zone is a magical place to be.'* He chose green paper, a gold gel pen, and set out his text using bubble writing for emphasis. He paid attention to design to help the reader. In the outside world design and image are central to the reading of text (Kress 1997). In writing for real inside the magical world of the Writing Zone, Anthony and other children in the class used this understanding to create texts in which design, image and text wove together to create meaning.

Anthony enjoyed the experience of writing in the Zone and wrote with enthusiasm. In fact all children in the class enjoyed writing in the Zone, and most produced powerful pieces of writing in these sessions. However, only two children at a time could work there, and Ann wondered how the excitement of writing in the Zone could be brought into the classroom. Some elements could not be replicated, for instance the cosiness of sitting tucked away in a special area. However, Ann realised that it was possible to bring choice of stationery and special pens into the classroom, and this was organised to the children's delight. In addition, the important element that could be replicated was that of choice: in the Zone children were free to choose what to write. Ann, like Tracey, decided to introduce writing journals to the whole class.

Writing Journals

Most children in the class loved the opportunity to choose what to write in their writing journals, and wrote powerfully. However, Anthony's entries were brief. One or two describe major life events, for instance, the arrival of a new bike and an account of a

> He was making expected progress in the transcriptional aspects of writing, but these concerns no longer dominated his thinking.

birthday party. There is one response to a letter from Ann in which he replies simply *'Thank you for your message'*. Otherwise, the journal entries are abandoned story retellings of traditional tales. How could Ann create a community in her classroom in which all children, including Anthony, saw themselves as writers and wrote with joy and enthusiasm?

Writing in role

Ann knew that children loved hearing stories read aloud. Writing briefly about characters from stories heard was a characteristic of writing in her classroom. She decided to try two further ways in which teachers had been successful in the first year of the Project: rehearsing writing through talk and writing in role. She planned to engage children in writing in the role of Philip, the timid 'wolf' in *Wolf Academy* (Allen 1997). She first invited children to work in pairs, talking to each other in role as Philip and his mum. All the children, except Anthony, were able to engage in paired role-play, and this talk helped them shape their subsequent writing. Anthony was paralysed with shyness, and unable to engage in talk with his partner. His subsequent written work does not sustain the voice of one character from the story. Instead it consists of snippets of the swirl of talk he heard around him as he sat frozen, unable to talk.

Writing from pictures

By this stage in the research, most children were writing with enjoyment and increased sophistication. The exception was Anthony, who came to life as a writer only during visits to the Writing Zone. Then one day Ann read the colourful picture book *Masha and the Firebird* to the class (Bateson-Hill 1999). She noticed that Anthony looked animated, and that he moved closer and closer to the book, to peer at the pictures. She wrote in her diary, *'I wonder if Anthony is unable to visualise images in his head?'* What would happen, she wondered, if she gave Anthony an image to write from? If he had a physical image in front of him, would he find it easier to write? She presented the class with a photo of a boy walking along a street, past closed doors. She invited children to talk in pairs about what they thought the boy might be feeling, and then to write brief ideas on post-it notes to stick around the photo. These ideas were shared. Next, children were invited to write in the first person as the boy. With the image in front of him Anthony could see the boy and so was able to enter into his world. For the first time Anthony wrote confidently in role in the first person.

Ann used this insight to inform her teaching. In a later piece of work based on *The After Dark Princess* (Dalton 1990), children worked first in pairs to rehearse their thinking through talk.

> Ann persevered and eventually found the key to Anthony's engagement as a writer.

Then they were invited to draw their own invented maps of Jo's quest. Finally, they were asked to write in role as Jo. This was to be Anthony's most powerful piece of writing. It begins *'I climbed the shiny stairs. But I knew I was being watched. As I climbed the swirly gold stairs I was worried about Alice…I was nearly at the top when the emperor of nightfall said "You are not welcome here…fear my wrath"*. Anthony had created an image on paper through drawing and so was able to write powerfully in the first person as Jo.

Conclusion

At the end of her research Ann invited the children to make brochures for Y2 advertising writing in Y3. Anthony wrote about the fun of writing from pictures. He ended his brochure with the words:
Y2 will have a blast
If you come in our class
At the beginning of the year Anthony had written about his unhappiness at having to write, and also elsewhere at his sadness at having no one to play with. Anthony's writing was now more assured, and it is clear from his brochure and from observations in the classroom that he was now confident in his classroom community. Ann persevered and eventually found the key to Anthony's engagement as a writer. She changed her teaching in the light of her perceptive observations and all her class made marked progress as writers. Overall 85 % of the class, including Anthony, moved on at least one level on the CLPE Writing Scale.

Year 6: Darren

The final story is about Darren, in Y6. His teacher, Gareth Evans was in his fourth year of teaching and had been newly appointed as Language Co-ordinator. His school is in an area of mixed private and council housing. Darren, of black Afro-Caribbean/ white European heritage, was chosen by Gareth to be his case study boy as he was a quiet child, who rarely contributed to class discussion. He enjoyed writing letters to relatives and friends at home, but in school considered that *'the most important thing about writing was spelling'*. It was predicted that he would be borderline 3/4 in the KS2 end of year assessment.

Reading aloud

Gareth thought hard about changes to teaching introduced by Writing Project colleagues. He decided to read aloud regularly to the children and changed his quiet reading into group sessions in which children read aloud and discussed favourite books and poems. Children and teacher began to enjoy reading.

Writing journals

Gareth also introduced writing journals. He decided to give children the choice of whether or not to share this writing. In his reflective journal he thought about the Y6 teacher who had introduced journals in the first year of the Project, *'I felt that the teacher must have had an awfully good relationship with her class. I was really quite envious and hoped I could be half as good...What if the children never trust me enough to read their journals?'* Despite these misgivings he persevered. Darren and most other children in the class enjoyed writing in their journals. Darren's entries surprised Gareth. He began to write a series of quite violent stories and letters. For instance, one imaginary letter begins, *'Dear Dad, I went to Crystal Palace Park. There was a robbery and the robber tried to kidnap me, but I moved too quickly and I kicked him 5 times then punched him 19 times and then he was down on the floor. Then I got a glass bottle and whacked it at him. There he was lying down with drippy blood.'* Gareth was surprised as in class and in the playground Darren was *'a meek little boy'*. In *The Cool Web* Harding (1977) claimed that stories give the reader the opportunity to explore imagined events vicariously. Darren used his Writing Journal as a safe place to invent and explore different ways of participating in imagined events.

Talking about writing

Gareth next considered another Project finding, and wondered 'would writing be better if children were allowed to talk?' Writing had always been done silently in his school, and he was concerned about how others would react, and whether some children would 'get nothing done at all?' He decided to invite children to talk about their writing in a unit of work about David Copperfield. He spent several days reading aloud from an abridged version. It was clear that children were totally involved in the story. Earlier in the year they had been introduced to the genre of interview writing and Gareth suggested that children create an interview with David Copperfield. He had himself written an interview in the style of the 'Esther' programme, and he showed and read this to the children. They were then invited to choose one or two people to work with. Without exception, all chose gender groupings.

Gareth observed Darren with Rob, his partner. Rob suggested they wrote their interview in the style of a 'Jerry' Programme, and went on to say 'I'll be Jerry, would you like to be David Copperfield?' Darren looked delighted, and the two boys began to brain-storm ideas for the interview. The children talked in role, and continued to do so as they wrote the interview itself on the computer. All children were completely focussed on the task. They wrote as experts as they knew the story well, knew how

Earlier in the year they had been introduced to the genre of interview writing and Gareth suggested that children create an interview with David Copperfield.

to write interviews, and were familiar with the Jerry Springer Show format. Children worked keenly, with excitement, and produced lively scripts in the style of the television genre. For instance, the one written by Rob and Darren begins,

Jerry: Hello, and welcome to a very special episode of Jerry Springer. Today we meet the famous man himself, DAVID COPPERFIELD!!!

(Audience clap, David enters)

Jerry: Was Mr. Murdstone nice to you?

David: He didn't like me and punished me horribly for it and sent me to boarding school

(Audience boo + Hiss)

Despite the lively twentieth-century television style, the character of David shines through the interview. For instance, Jerry continues:

Jerry: Sorry to ask this, but how were your feelings when you were told your mother had died?

In composing the script Darren thought hard when asked this question. There was a silence, and then he replied:
David: I felt like any other boy would, a horrible sensation inside.

Darren was able to explore his thinking in role with a trusted friend but Gareth wondered whether he would be able to share this writing with the whole class? He had never before volunteered to do so. Gareth welcomed children to the Jerry Springer show and invited children to contribute. Darren and Rob were among the first to volunteer. They walked, in role, to the front of the class and Rob introduced himself confidently as Jerry Springer. Darren then turned to the class, and beckoned them to clap and cheer. He went on to read his interview answers confidently, and continued to encourage his audience to clap or boo in the appropriate places. Darren and Rob performed the writing and clearly enjoyed the response from the class.

Conclusion

Through hearing texts read aloud, writing in his Writing Journal, working in role with partners of his own choice, and experiencing genuine response his reading aloud, Darren began to develop strong voices in his writing. For instance, in role as David he wrote a powerful love letter to Dora. In his final interview he stated, *'I don't worry so much now with my spelling and handwriting.'* Despite this, his spelling did improve as he became a more confident, joyful writer. Overall, 81% of the class, including Darren, moved on at least one level on the CLPE Writing Scale. In addition, all the class achieved a Level 4 in the KS2 English SATS.

Top Floor Flat
18, Adelphi Street
London
WC1
12th February 1850

Dearest Dora,
        It has only been a few hours since I
saw you. I have missed you a lot. I really ~~miss~~ enjoyed
our picnic even though I wanted to ask you something I loved
the bit when I kissed your hand. I still can't keep my mind of
you ~~so~~ ever since the first time I saw you. It was ~~nice~~ lovely
when we got engaged*I can't stop thinking about it. I want
to ask you now if you want to marry me my lovely dearest Dora
I would like you to tell me when we meet again.

                            Love from ~~David~~
                            David

Changes to teaching

What were the changes made by these four teachers that made such a difference to children's confidence and competence as writers?

Fun in teaching

First, we need to look at the teachers themselves. What is marked is the extent to which they enjoyed the challenge of being creative teachers, and had fun in their teaching. I think this is significant. We were all caught up in Carol's enthusiasm for her Dinosaur Den, Tracey's fun in story telling, Ann's delight in her Writing Zone, and Gareth's joy in 'David Copperfield meets Jerry Springer'.

Excitement is catching. Children caught the excitement and wrote with enjoyment. Because writing was fun they began to choose to write. Through having fun in writing I think the four teachers enabled children to see themselves as writers. Because children saw themselves as writers they were receptive to teaching about writing and so made marked progress as writers.

Perseverance

The extent to which the teachers persevered is also striking. For week after week Carol brought to the group her despair that, although other boys were taking on her ideas for writing in imaginative play, Greg was simply not choosing to write. Eventually, significantly, she was to discover that Greg was in fact a storyteller. Her scribing of his scientific observations in the Dinosaur Den, and of his imaginative contributions to the group story about dinosaurs, led him to begin to make links between the stories in his head and marks on paper.

Ann's determination was also remarkable.

> Through having fun in writing I think the four teachers enabled children to see themselves as writers.

Through the changes she made to her teaching all children except Anthony began to make real progress as writers. Another teacher in the group, Penny Orme (Orme 2001) had discovered that it was important for many children, particularly boys, to draw characters from the stories they were creating. Listening to children as they worked, it was clear that the characters were coming to life for them as they drew. Ann picked up and adapted this finding. She realised that Anthony could be helped by working from pictures. With a picture in front of him, he too could write powerfully in role in the first person.

Common Patterns

The four classes cover a wide age range, from Reception to Y6. Despite this, patterns of teaching are similar in each of the four classes. The teachers' enjoyment of the challenge of being creative teachers, and determination to move all children on as writers, are key to children's significant achievement as writers. In addition, each of the four class teachers:

- enjoyed reading children's books, and read aloud to children often, and with enthusiasm
- entered imagined worlds with their children, through story telling and drama
- encouraged children to write in role in the first person
- gave children time to work on their thinking before writing: through talk, drawing and drama
- invited children to choose what to write in Writing Journals
- gave children opportunities to work with children of their own choice: this often involved boys working with boys and girls with girls
- gave children opportunities to praise and encourage each other by talking informally about writing in progress
- made opportunities for children to work collaboratively on pieces of writing with children of their own choice
- encouraged children to bring home lives and popular culture into the classroom, and to talk and write about these interests
- encouraged children to read aloud their writing to each, and to the whole class

These findings were replicated in classes in which children made the greatest overall progress in writing in the second year of the Project. At the end of second year we were again delighted to find that 72% of the children had moved on at least one level on the CLPE Writing Scale. The difference between boys and girls was not marked - 73% of girls and 71% of boys had moved on. This indicates that the teaching was effective for both girls and boys.

It is not a coincidence that many of these findings replicate those of Barrs and Cork

(2001). We were excited to hear about the work of the CLPE Project which gave us confidence to make reading aloud to children a significant part of everyday practice. We were also interested in the centrality of drama in supporting children's writing, and ways in which it helped children to write powerfully in role. We too found that 'public readings' of children's writing were important to young writers, in enabling them to hear the tunes and rhythms of their writing, and giving them opportunities to see the effect of their writing on trusted audiences.

Our finding about boys choosing to work with boys and girls with girls is interesting. Boys as well as girls wrote powerfully within same-gender groupings. The idea of giving children choice about writing companions is a marked change from accepted practice in many classrooms. This is a finding we intend to continue to research over the next two years.

We were interested to hear Elaine Millard and Jackie Marsh talk to us about the centrality of popular culture in children's literacy learning. This replicated our own observations of the ways in which many children wrote in their Writing Journals. The use of Writing Journals has spread, and this year we have begun a separate Writing Journal Research Project sponsored by the United Kingdom Reading Association (UKRA).

The achievement of black boys

The achievement of black (mainly Caribbean) boys this year is significant; 82% moved on at least one level on the Scale. In the first year of the Project black boys were the least achieving group, in the second they were the highest. What made a difference?

Interest

In the second year of the Project a significant number of teachers selected black boys as case study children. Discussion in Project Inset focused on teachers' observations of these children in relation to new ways of teaching writing. Much of the discussion in the second year therefore highlighted the progress of black boys as writers. Black boys were noticed.

Although changes to teaching are tried with all children in the class, the nature of the Project means that teachers are particularly aware of the effect of these changes on their case study children. In most instances, case study children warm to this interest. Indeed, during the last six years of action research in Croydon, a few case study children became keen readers and writers almost overnight because they realised that their teacher was genuinely interested in their progress. In the second year of the Project, black boys warmed to the interest being shown by their Project teachers.

...during the last six years of action research in Croydon, a few case study children became keen readers and writers almost overnight because they realised that their teacher was genuinely interested in their progress.

Expectations

It is expected that teachers will move their case study children on as writers. The Project involves researching new ways of teaching writing and monitoring the effect of these changes with particular reference to the case study children. In the action research model, teachers keep trying until ways of successful teaching are discovered. There was an expectation that teachers would find ways of moving these children on as writers. The teachers persevered, and they did. Black boys made significant progress.

New ways of teaching

Given these factors, were there marked differences in the teaching of writing in the first and second years of the Project? If so, are the discoveries made in the second year of particular importance to black boys?

In the second year teachers built on findings from the first (Graham 2001). They had discovered that it was important to read aloud frequently, to make opportunities for children to write as experts and about what mattered to them. They encouraged children to work in companionship with each other (particularly boys with boys), to read writing aloud and to experience genuine response to their writing from peers. All these factors were found to be important in the second year of the Project.

Some changes to teaching were new in the second year, and may have been instrumental in moving black boys on as writers. In the second year teachers themselves created and engaged with children in imagined worlds. Carol and Ann each physically created an imaginative space in the classroom: the dinosaur den and the writing zone. Tracey created an imaginative space through the stories she invented, and Gareth through writing and role play: his written *Esther* interview and his spoken introduction to the Jerry Springer show. Children were encouraged to work collaboratively, to choose their companions, to read aloud as they wrote, and to perform their writing to the class at the end of the session. I have a vivid picture of three boys, one white and two black, working together in this classroom. They chose to sprawl on the floor as they composed the first draft, and were engrossed, trying out snippets to see how they sounded and arguing about appropriate layout. They relished the opportunity to word-process and print out their final version, humming as they did so, one boy sighing and saying *'this is the life!'* They then performed the scene to the class with verve and panache (Organ 2001).

In our reading project the most successful teachers *'shared their own affective reactions to texts with the children'* (Barrs 2000). This then made it possible for children to express their own responses freely, and to engage at an emotional level in their reading. Reading is about responding, and writing about making. In the second year of the writing project, teachers themselves began to make and enter imagined worlds with their children. This then made it possible for children themselves to begin to create their own imagined worlds, through writing.

Lynda Graham
Professional Development Consultant for English.
London Borough of Croydon.

Project teachers Year 2 1999-2001
Patricia Ansley, Elaine Burley, Carol Domingo, Sarah Ellis, Gareth Evans, Geraldine Field, Linda Ford, Debbie Garrido, Sarah Hayward, Fe Hurst, Ann Hudson, Annette Johnson, Tracey Maddick, Stefania Mitchell, Abigail Newell, Tracey Newvell, Linda O'Callaghan, Collette Organ, Penny Orme, Emma Packam, Pat Parlour, Caroline Rosie, Tina Saturno, Emilie Stirling, Jenny Thorne, Clare Warne

Thanks are due to the English team who spread ideas from the Writing Project across the borough. They are Sue Frater, (Inspector for English), Jacqui Pick (Advisor for English) and Pauline Thomson, Hilary Grainger, Elizabeth Blake (National Literacy Strategy Consultants).

References

Barrs, Myra & Cork,Valerie(2001) *The Reader in the Writer* London, Centre for Language in Primary Education

Barrs, Myra (2000) 'Gendered Literacy' *Language Arts* 77(4)

Boomer, Garth (1985) *Fair Dinkum Teaching and Learning* New Jersey, Boynton/Cook

Bruner, Jerome (1986) *Actual Minds, Possible Worlds* London, Harvard University Press

CLPE (1997) *Writing Scales 1 & 2* London, Centre for Language in Primary Education

Chambers, Aidan (1993) *Tell Me* Stroud, The Thimble Press

Fox, Carol (1993) *At the Very Edge of the Forest* London, Cassell

Graham, Lynda (1999) 'Changing Practice through Reflection: the KS2 Reading Project, Croydon' *Reading* 33(3) p.106

Graham, Lynda (2001) 'From Tyrannosaurus to Pokemon: Autonomy in the Teaching of Writing *Reading* 35(1) p.18

Grainger, Teresa & Cremin, Mark (2001) *Resourcing Classroom Drama: 5-8* Sheffield, NATE

Graves, Donald (1983) *Writing* Heinemann Educational Books

Harding, D W (1977) 'What happens when we read?' in Meek, Margaret, Warlow, Aidan &

Barton, Griselda, eds. *The Cool Web* London, The Bodley Head

Johnson, Annette (2000) 'The importance of oracy in developing children's writing' unpublished dissertation for the diploma in Writing and Action Research, Davidson Professional Centre, Croydon

Kress, Gunther (1997) *Before Writing* London, Routledge

Lambirth, Andrew (1997) 'Juicy Bits: developing a taste for poetry' in Barrs, Myra & Rosen, Michael, eds. *A Year with Poetry* London, Centre for Language in Primary Education

McClusky, Heidi (1999) 'Writers Block' unpublished dissertation for the diploma in Writing and Action Research, Davidson Professional Centre, Croydon

Marsh, Jackie (2001) 'One-Way Traffic? Connections Between Literacy Practices at home and in the nursery' University of Sheffield Research topic Papers

Marsh, Jackie & Millard,Elaine (2000) *Literacy and Popular Culture* London, Paul Chapman Publishing

Medwell, Jane, Wray, David, Poulson, Louise & Fox, Richard (1998) *Effective Teachers of Literacy*, commissioned by the Teacher Training Agency. Exeter, University of Exeter

Organ, Colette (2000) unpublished diploma dissertation

Orme, P. (2000) unpublished portfolio, Advanced Certificate in writing and action research, Canterbury Christchurch University College

Wells, Gordon (1986) *The Meaning Makers* London, Hodder and Stoughton

Books for children

Agard, John & Nicholas, Grace, eds. (1996) *A Caribbean Dozen* London, Walker

Allen, Jonathan (1997) *Wolf Academy* London,Orchard Books

Bateson-Hill, Margaret & Wilson, Anne (1999) *Masha and the Firebird* Slough, Zero to Ten

Dalton, Annie (1990, 2001) *The Afterdark Princess*, London Mammoth

Hayes, Sarah (1986) *This is the Bear* London, Walker

Piers, Helen & Foreman, Michael (1982) *Long Neck and Thunder Foot* London, Kestrel

Rosen, Michael (1996) *Mind Your Own Business* London, Scholastic

> Reading is about responding, and writing about making. In the second year of the writing project, teachers themselves began to make and enter imagined worlds with their children.

CHAPTER 9

An interest in what non-fiction is and how it is taught in school leads Gemma Moss to look at one child's construction of a non-fiction text, and its links to published texts, and to consider how the relationship between word and image in information books can be used to help structure pupils' non-fiction writing.

Explicit pedagogy

Gemma Moss

Within education circles, one key assumption that underpins much thinking on boys and literacy attainment is that boys prefer non-fiction genres. In some quarters this leads to the construction of the following argument. That the historical prevalence of fiction on the primary school curriculum has acted against boys' interests, and that consequently a stronger diet of non-fiction will lead to improvements in both their reading and writing. Some have seen the shift in emphasis towards non-fiction genres in the National Literacy Strategy as evidence of attempts to produce a more boy-friendly curriculum along these lines.

In fact, when looked at more closely, boys' association with non-fiction looks more tenuous than might at first appear. When I ran a research project designed to track the formation of gendered preferences in reading in the junior age group, it swiftly became apparent that the bulk of the reading diet children chose for themselves was fiction. Boys who exercised a clear preference for non-fiction were a particular sub-group – mainly those whom the school designated as less proficient readers – and the non-fiction texts they chose were non-fiction texts with a high density of pictures, which could be used to steer the reader through the text without recourse to much of the writing (Moss, 2000; Moss & Attar, 1999). Further confirmation of this point of view came from a study of children's library borrowing I recently conducted, analysing the borrowing records of a three form Year 6 group, collected over a one year period. The group of roughly 90 children consisted of two thirds boys, yet only 17% of the borrowings were non-fiction, and only 4% of the borrowers borrowed more non-fiction than fiction - all boys with a designation of special educational needs. Reviewing the quantitative data on children's

> ...when looked at more closely boys' association with non-fiction books looks more tenuous than in might first appear.

book choice in this light, it becomes apparent that non-fiction reading is very much a minority preference, but that boys constitute a majority of this minority. Extrapolating from this latter data produces the myth of boys' absolute preference for non-fiction.

Where does this leave the literacy curriculum? At least in part what it does is highlight the responsibility schools have for introducing non-fiction forms to both boys and girls: non-fiction needs to be made accessible to everybody in the class. But the research outlined above also raises questions about what we take non-fiction to be. It has led me to re-examine how we categorise and think about non-fiction, and to move away from definitions solely based on subject content or linguistic text type. Instead I have begun to think about non-fiction texts as offering different kinds of reading experience by deploying words and images in different proportions, and as being textually organised in different ways (Moss, 2001). In this article I will argue that such a shift in conception has implications for how we support boys' (and girls') non-fiction writing, and put forward some new approaches to working with non-fiction texts in the classroom.

"Make a booklet": one child's struggle with a writing task

I start with an actual example of a writing task, stemming from a Year 6 classroom. The writer is an able boy, placed in a literacy group aiming at Level 5 in their SATs. In the term in which the data was collected, the class had been studying the Egyptians as part of the history curriculum. They had undertaken a number of supported tasks in the whole class, designed to consolidate information retrieval skills, such as selective reading and note-taking, and the use of notes to draft a final piece of writing. The particular task I describe here was a culmination of this kind of activity.

The direction the teacher gave was that the class should make a booklet on an Egyptian theme. This involved choosing their own topics, followed by time and internet access in which to assemble the information they needed on them in their rough books, prior to producing the final piece. Writing-up was undertaken as homework, for which each child had been provided with a blank sheet of A4.

The topic Thomas had chosen was mummification. He was pleased to have found rather a lot about this on the various websites he'd visited, and he had had no trouble making notes. But making the booklet proved more bothersome. Right from the outset he could see that this involved having to fill rather a lot of space - two sides of A4 to be exact - and he wasn't sure exactly how he would manage this. At this point, Thomas conceptualised the processes involved in completing the task as transferring the information from the notebook onto the sheet *"I have all the information I need. It's in my rough book, I've just got to get it from here to there."* With a reminder that the task could involve both words and pictures, he set about it.

"*When Egyptian civilization began*"; "*Later on the Egyptians*"; and "*After many centuries*". In between the first two paragraphs he drew two long lines about 4 centimetres apart and inserted a small drawing, showing a dead body lying in the sand surrounded by grave goods, with two animals moving in on the carcass. At the bottom of the page, in a similar space, he drew a line of canopic jars. Turning over, the next booklet page is much more closely filled with written text, with just a two centimetre gap at the bottom, showing a small cartoon of grave robbers at work. In fact, on this booklet page, only the first paragraph is about mummifying. It begins with the phrase, "*Next the body was covered in crystals*", and then goes on to describe what would happen to the body after it had been embalmed, when it was laid in a coffin. Having apparently run out of things to say about mummification, Thomas then changes the topic to tombs. Accordingly, the second paragraph begins with: "*There were several types of tombs*"; whilst the final paragraph on this page starts with "*Now for the most famous tombs*".

By the bottom of the second booklet page, Thomas has already produced a considerable amount of information about the Egyptians, mummification and their style of tombs, but he is still only halfway through the given space.

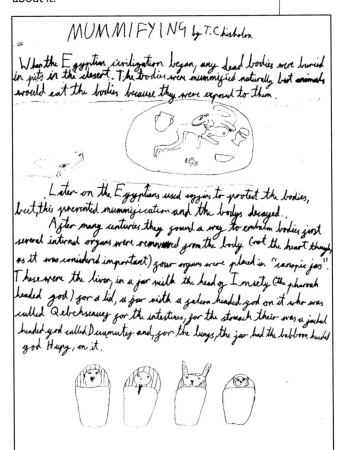

First the A4 page was folded down the middle, creating four A5 sections, or booklet pages. Then Thomas began the writing by placing at the top of the first A5 section the title: Mummifying. Underneath, the opening page contains three paragraphs which in turn begin:

Perhaps as a direct consequence, on the last two A5 sections, the space taken up by the writing shrinks whilst the pictures expand. On the penultimate booklet page, a single paragraph beginning "*The final type of tomb*" sits at the top of the A5 section. The remaining

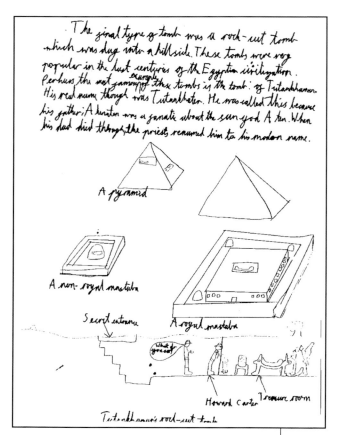

The final type of tomb was a rock-cut tomb which was dug into a hillside. These tombs were very popular in the last centuries of the Egyptian civilization. Perhaps the most famous of these tombs is the tomb of Tutankhamun. His real name though was Tutankhaten. He was called this because his father Akhenaten was a fanatic about the sun god Aten. When his dad died through the priests renamed him to his modern name.

A pyramid

A non-royal mastaba

Secret entrance

A royal mastaba

Howard Carter

Treasure room

Tutankhamun's rock-cut tomb

space is given over to a sequence of pictures of tombs, arranged in a circular fashion, in the middle of the page. Beneath them, running horizontally across the remaining space, there is a diagram showing a cross-section of Tutankhamen's tomb, complete with staircase, antechamber and treasure room. The final booklet page consists of one short paragraph, beginning *"In some tombs you can find"*, followed

In some tombs you can find clay slaves put in them to help the deceased in the afterlife they took orders from Osiris, god of the dead. They each held a tool and an inscription from the book of the dead. They were called Shabti and looked like this.

Here some gods that helped the dead and mummifying

Anubis
Embalming

Osiris
god of the dead

Thoth
whispered to the dead

by a very large picture of a clay slave, or Shabti, which takes up roughly half the page. Then there is a single closing sentence *"Here some gods that helped the dead and mummifying"* (sic) followed by three much smaller pictures of the gods, standing in a line.

In describing the final product in the way in which I have, I have suggested that the task, "Make a booklet", presented itself to this child as a problem of filling space. Working through the task this problem became increasingly acute as he gradually used up his store of information. The text lends itself to being analysed in this way because of the relationship between the writing and the pictures – the way in which one shrinks as the other expands; and the development of the theme, including the sharp switch from "mummifying" to "tombs". Keeping the focus just at this level, there are a number of potentially quite straightforward solutions to this child's writing problems. If the space was really too large for a single topic, then the task specification should have been changed accordingly – same space, more topics, or stick to one topic and reduce the space. Alternatively, this could be seen as a planning problem, in which things got out of hand because the child couldn't anticipate as he started the piece, what would happen later. More experience of planning for both pictures and written text ahead of writing, rather than launching straight from notes, would be an obvious answer. These kinds of interventions preserve intact how we think about writing non-fiction: what seems to need minor adjustment is the specification of the particular task.

However, I want to argue that once we start taking seriously the way in which compositions happen within a finite, rather than an indefinitely expanding, space, and recognise that this impacts, however directly or indirectly, on the structure of the text itself, we shall also need to adjust how we think about non-fiction writing and the best ways of supporting it.

The struggle for order in non-fiction writing

To develop this argument further, I will return first of all to Thomas' text. In my initial analysis I identified the contents of his writing, and its organisation, by quoting from the opening sentence of each paragraph in turn. This gives the following sequence:

1 *"When the Egyptian civilization began..."*
2 *"Later on the Egyptians used"*
3 *"After many centuries they found"*
4 *"Next the body was covered"*
5 *"There were several types of tomb"*
6 *"Now for the most famous tombs"*
7 *"The final type of tomb was"*
8 *"In some tombs you can find"*
9 *"Here [are] some gods that helped the dead and mummifying"*

As paragraph openers these do pretty well. Change the overall title of the piece to "Egyptians and the Dead", so that the processes of mummification *and* place of burial both have equal relevance, and the whole reads as sharply focused and sequenced right down to the final sentence. (The piece could almost act as an exemplar for a judicious writing frame.) Yet look beyond the opening sentence to what happens next within the paragraph, and the writer's struggle to establish cohesion in the text becomes much more apparent. Indeed, it becomes possible to see that the strength of the temporal frame: "When"; "Later"; "After"; "Next" as applied to mummification is in some ways precisely leading this writer into the difficulties he has in filling the given space. These phrases indicate two implicit time frames functioning in the text here as organising principles – a) a contrast between how mummification took place in early, then later Egyptian society; and b) the sequence of actions which constitute mummification and burial. All the notes that Thomas has made on mummification, and what he understands about different aspects of the process, have to be compressed into this sequence. What won't fit into a "first of all/ later" frame gets squeezed out in order to preserve this overall structure.

Later on in the text, the opening sentence exercises less of a hold over the contents of the paragraph, as the author seems to cast around much more for ways of filling the space. So paragraph 7 reads in its entirety like this:

The final type of tomb was a rock-cut tomb which was dug into a hillside. These tombs were very popular in the last centuries of the Egyptian civilization. Perhaps the most famous example of these tombs is the tomb of Tutankhamen. His real name was Tutankhaten. He was called this because his father, Akenaten was a fanatic about the sun-god Aten. When his dad died though the priests renamed him to his modern name.

In a way this paragraph raises quite sharply the question of what our expectations should be of the text forms that children are being asked to produce. The higher profile given to non-fiction genres in the National Literacy Strategy, and the close specification of their textual organisation make clear that the ideal for this text type is a maximally cohesive structure, where the parts are clearly subjugated to the whole. To this end the National Literacy Strategy has emphasised the importance of conjunctions and connectives, viewing these as the linguistic glue which holds text types together, an approach which owes much to genre theory. Similarly, the EXEL tradition, exemplified through writing frames, sees as pivotal to grasping text structure the organisation of information into a closely woven sequence, in which the opening line of each paragraph plays a key role.

In *Grammar for Writing* this kind of approach

> The current vocabularies for describing non-fiction text types – report; explanation; exposition – bring to mind texts composed of well-crafted continuous prose.

makes an appearance as the "one paragraph per box principle" (p93) Information is segmented into its unifying parts, the parts are sequenced into a coherent whole. The National Literacy Strategy framework re-iterates this view of the role paragraphs play within a longer text through the termly specification of teaching objectives. In Year 4 Term 2, for instance, one objective is "to identify how and why paragraphs are used to organise and sequence information". In Year 6 Term 3 the objective is "to divide whole texts into paragraphs, paying attention to the sequence of paragraphs and to the links between one paragraph and the next eg. through the choice of appropriate connectives".

Yet the ideal text type being invoked here is far removed from a good many of the non-fiction sources that the children themselves are most likely to be reading in class.

Non-fiction and the rise of the double-spread

The current vocabularies for describing non-fiction text types – report; explanation; exposition – bring to mind texts composed of well-crafted continuous prose. The separate specifications for each text-type are derived exclusively from analysis of their linguistic features. But many, if not most, of the non-fiction texts available in classrooms are carefully crafted composites of written text and image in which the writing is often directly shaped by the space it can occupy on the page (See Moss, 2001). Indeed the part it plays in the text as a whole may be subordinate to the image.

Dorling Kindersley's *Eye openers: Minibeasts* (Royston, 1992), for instance, gains its thematic unity by constructing the text as a series of double-spreads each of which contains exactly the same elements: a large heading top left, naming that double-spread's minibeast; a margin design running across the top of the page encompassing a sequence of drawings of the minibeast in action; a large, centrally-placed photograph of the minibeast; written labels, and hand-drawn close-ups of parts of the minibeast; an additional drawing of the minibeast in its habitat; small drawings of the minibeast next to the page numbers; and a paragraph describing what the minibeast does.

The paragraph here interacts with the pictures to establish the theme. It does not do the job on its own. This subordination of the text to the image is symptomatic of Dorling Kindersley's publications as a whole. In their text design, written paragraphs often follow and accompany the image, rather than vice-versa. This leads to a much looser text structure, where the reading path is not determined by a fixed sequence to the order in which individual paragraphs will be read. Rather each reader is free to create their own reading path, as they browse around the given elements on a page, in the order they choose this time. Accordingly, the paragraph itself begins to play a different role in the context of the text as a whole.

The paragraph floats free

The kind of text design represented by Dorling Kindersley's *Eyewitness Guides* has now been much imitated by other publishers of junior age non-fiction (Moss, 2001). As a result it is becoming increasingly rare to find a double spread in which the topic is developed through the judicious sequencing of one paragraph after another, tightly tied into a single closely ordered piece of writing. Instead, each of the paragraphs on a given page is more likely to function as a self-sufficient unit, loosely aggregated into a thematic whole in a number of different ways. For instance, in the Kingfisher *I wonder why..*series, *I wonder why Spiders Spin Webs* includes a double-spread on which the following questions, boldly printed, are used to signal some of the paragraph contents: *"Which ants live in a tent?"; "Whose house has a trapdoor?"; "Whose nest is paper thin?"* (O'Neill, 1995, p22). Without explicitly announcing it, the main conceptual theme here is the different ways in which insects can make themselves homes. The reader is left to infer this, however, from the combination of available words and pictures. Linguistic cohesion between the paragraphs rests solely on the syntactic repetition in the opening sentences of the answers: *"The trapdoor spider's burrow has a door...." "The paper wasp's nest has paper walls..." "A tent caterpillar spins a shady silk canopy.." "Termites are champion builders".*

What does this all have to do with children's non-fiction writing, let alone how teachers might best support it? Looking at non-fiction in this way forces us to re-conceptualise what non-fiction writing is and how it works. It underlines that fact that non-fiction texts often work by using a combination of words and pictures, within a given space to establish their theme. It also makes us re-define the potential role of the paragraph in these kinds of texts. For each paragraph may well establish its place in the larger text through reference to the images, rather than the other paragraphs which have preceded or followed it. Recognising these different ways of organising larger textual units, I will argue, allows us to develop new means of supporting children's developing skills as non-fiction writers.

The paragraph on the page

I have been suggesting that we reconsider the paragraph and the place it occupies on the non-fiction page, by concentrating on those texts where it is designed to be read alongside and in varying combination with a range of other chunks of written text and images. In this kind of

Recognising these different ways of organising larger textual units, allows us to develop new means of supporting children's developing skills as non-fiction writers.

non-fiction text the physical space of the double-spread becomes the underlying organising principle; the distribution of the chunks of written text and images on the page announces the theme. What are the consequences of this view for supporting non-fiction writing?

Firstly, it gives a new prominence to the free-standing paragraph, considered as a unit in its own right. This provides a new focus for teaching. In some contexts it may indeed be appropriate to continue to teach the paragraph, as a way of subdividing a longer piece of text. But it also becomes possible to use the free-standing paragraph as a mini text, and a teaching end in itself. In fact, the free-standing paragraph in the kind of non-fiction texts I have been discussing, often operates as a concise model of genres such as the report or explanation. In the space of a few sentences, such paragraphs can provide useful examples of genre-specifications i.e. for the report, the move from general classification to a description of particular characteristics, using the present tense with generalised participants. Here is the paragraph on ants from *Eye-openers: Minibeasts*:

> *Wood ants live in a big nest on the ground. Each ant has its own job to do. Some ants look after the eggs and keep the nest tidy. Others search for food in the woods. They carry insects back to the nest to feed the young ants.* (Royston, 1992. p16)

Because they are so concise, these kinds of paragraphs lend themselves to a problem-solving approach: generating the principles upon which a particular example is built; looking for other examples which either fulfill, or perhaps lead one to alter those principles. The hunt for an exemplifying paragraph can thus underpin class reading of a wide range of non-fiction: looking for other examples which are the same; collecting other examples which are different. All of this can act as preparation for children's own writing, through providing plenty of opportunities for children to familiarise themselves with "the text's tunes" (Barrs, 1992). The teacher is in the position to widen or narrow the scope of the point of comparison, depending upon the choice of texts used for this kind of activity and the divergent or convergent principles they use to shape their paragraph structure.

Secondly, the kinds of non-fiction texts I have been focusing on open up a range of possibilities for thinking about the thematic relationship between picture and written text, and vice versa. What kind of picture would best illustrate the paragraph about ants quoted above, for instance? Where there is more than one possibility, what grounds can children muster for using one picture rather than another? If there is space on the page for more than one picture, which should be the largest, which the smallest?

I have used this kind of exercise with adult audiences to open up questions about thematic unity, and how it is achieved. Taking four assorted paragraphs from a single non-fiction page spread, without identifying the source, I have asked the audience to sequence them in as many ways as possible, then decide on one version, add headings and finally imagine the best image to accompany their text. This leads to very different versions of what the final text might look like, all constructed from the same set of paragraphs. The last such session produced the following range of headings from the same paragraphs about life in Finland: "The Saame People"; "Life at the Top of the World"; "Polar Nights", and "Eleven Year-old Ari". In each case, very different images had been chosen as ways of consolidating the thematic unity for each group's version. One group suggested an image of the globe, with an arrow pointing to Finland, as they had put a high priority on the geographical information the writing contained. The woman who suggested Polar Nights as the title wanted a poetic image of the setting sun, emphasising what it would be like to live somewhere with so much winter darkness. Another group had focused in on a paragraph containing a child's reported speech and highlighted that personal voice by choosing an image of the speaker. The ordering of the text, its signposting through headings and accompanying images, makes for a different understandings of the main theme and its constituent parts, even though the actual paragraphs remain the same.

This kind of exercise can be taken two ways. On the one hand, it shows that paragraphs which are only loosely integrated on the page, can be integrated more fully through amendment or addition. Because the bulk of the text already exists in this kind of exercise, children's conceptual thinking is freed to concentrate on how thematic unity can be produced in different ways, without them simultaneously struggling to control their own writing. On the other hand, approaching the substance of non-fiction in this way also offers the possibility of using the loose aggregation of paragraphs on the page as a valid means of textual organisation in its own right. I would argue that this can act as a valuable precursor to fully linear writing, where the text must be organised through the sequential ordering of the written text alone.

If loose aggregation of paragraphs were the goal, then one could imagine, in the context of Thomas' piece on mummification, that he could plan his writing less as a sequential unfolding of ideas than as a series of localised connections between words and images. The picture of canopic jars, for instance, has the potential to lead towards two rather different organising ideas: on the one hand they were the containers used to store particular internal organs which

...the way in which the double-spread establishes its thematic unity is as much to do with the choice of pictures ....as it is to do with close connections made between the units.

were stripped from the body as it was prepared for mummification. This potentially feeds into a description of the processes of mummification, and the risks of putrefaction which it set out to address. But the canopic jars *also* carry the images of some of the Egyptian gods, signalling a potentially separate topic – which in this kind of context could be left relatively free-standing, without the need to be fully integrated.

Images structuring texts

This brings me to my third point, the possibility of supporting non-fiction writing, through using images as the props which structure the text. Of course, in the context of the infant school, teachers are well-versed in using the child's drawing to support initial writing, so that in the first instance the picture suggests the written text which will accompany it. In Science, too, diagrams can be used to help children express conceptual ideas. The proposition I am putting forward here is that the way in which the double-spread establishes its thematic unity is as much to do with the choice of pictures which are brought into association there, as it is to do with close connections made between the units of written text. Take the *Eyewitness Guides: Ancient Rome*. At their best, the *Eyewitness Guides* operate as a kind of mini-tour of the collections of our largest national museums. It as if the drawers were being opened before our eyes and the objects to be found there put on display. Thus the *Eyewitness Guides: Ancient*

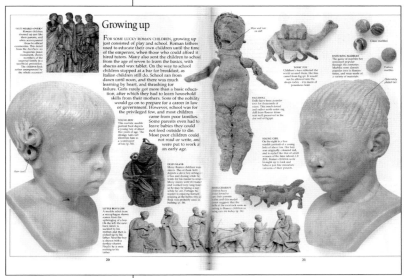

Rome, contains a range of archaeological artefacts, assembled as double-spreads to illustrate different aspects of Roman life and customs. The particular theme is established through the selection of images, and the accompanying written text. For the double-spread entitled "Growing up", for instance, the artefacts include a selection of Roman children's toys: marbles, a toy chariot and a rag doll; as well as some objects chosen because they illustrate what Roman children wore (depicted on a Roman frieze) or what they did (an oil lamp in the shape of a dozing child slave).

I have used this double-spread to act as the starting off-point for the following piece of image-led writing. If what we know about children's lives in Ancient Rome depends upon the array of objects presented on that page, what kinds of archaeological evidence might survive from the current generation into the future to tell about children's lives at the beginning of the second millennium? What kinds of images could be used to tell this tale? I and my children thought about this last summer as preparation for an in-service session I was conducting, and to this end, using a variety of internet websites, downloaded the following images:

A Lego bionicle figure;	a Pokemon card;
a lunchbox and flask;	a mobile phone; a Barbie;
a school rucksack;	a Gameboy;
a beanie babie;	a trainer; a roller blade.

Using desktop publishing software, the images were all made roughly the same size and fitted onto a single side of A4. The task I was then able to give the (adult) workshop participants was to choose which of the images they would include on an A3 double spread, to represent children's lives at the turn of the millennium. They were also asked to reflect on what they would leave out, and what else they might want to add in. Then they were invited to decide on how their chosen images would be laid out, with what headings, which would be the largest (and therefore most salient) images, and which the smallest.

This range of images suggests a number of competing themes which can be either accentuated or downplayed, according to their selection and depending on how they are then treated on the page, both in relation to each other and to the accompanying written text. Putting the Lego figure up against Barbie potentially brings up the topic of the gendering of children's toys; making the mobile phone the central image calls the age range into question. Using a desktop publishing package to handle this task makes images and written text instantly available for manipulation in different kinds of ways, and gives a point and purpose to writing with the aid of computer technology.

I have briefly sketched out what an image-led writing task might look like, keeping the emphasis on the processes of selection. I believe this encourages writers to think about:
- the choice of images which will be brought into association with each other;
- the ways in which they can be arranged on the page to emphasise different angles;
- how themes can be strengthened through the use of headings;
- how different aspects to the theme can be accentuated through the accompanying written text.

...many non-fiction texts are designed as composites of words and pictures, in which paragraphing plays a very different structural role

In undertaking this kind of work, my preference is to use actual examples of real texts as a reference point to steer and guide children's imagination, but at the same time provide them with a task which allows for many different ways of writing up. It is quite easy to adjust the level of support for these kinds of tasks by providing more or less of the input and a weaker or looser specification for the resulting writing.

Conclusion

In this article I have been arguing that many non-fiction texts are now designed as composites of words and pictures, in which the paragraph plays a very different structural role, released from its careful sequencing within a longer written text. This has led me to explore different ways of supporting the development of non-fiction writing, which can recognise and make use of these looser forms of textual organisation. I would argue that the kinds of ideas I have been outlining above bear a closer relationship to many boys' actual experience of reading non-fiction texts (Moss, 2000). Made available across the whole class, they also become a way of supporting all children's reading and writing of non-fiction, without leaving them to deal with the problem of imposing linear textual structure on diverse material as the first step in constructing non-fiction texts.

Gemma Moss
Institute of Education, London

References:
Barrs, Myra (1992) 'The Tune on the Page.' In Kimberley, Keith, Meek, Margaret and Miller, Jane (eds) *New Readings: Contributions to an understanding of literacy.* London: A&C Black

Children's Literature Research Centre. (1996) *Young people's reading at the end of the century.* London: Roehampton Institute

Coles, Martin & Hall, Christine (2002) 'Gendered readings: learning from children's reading choices.' In *Journal of Research in Reading.* Vol 25:1, 96-108

DfEE (2000) *Grammar for Writing.* London: DfEE

James, S. (1990) *Eyewitness Guides: Ancient Rome.* London: Dorling Kindersley

Kindersley, Barnabas & Anabel (1995) *Children just like me.* London: Dorling Kindersley

Moss, Gemma (2000) 'Raising boys' attainment in reading.' In *Reading* Vol 34:3, 101-106p

Moss, Gemma (2001) 'To Work or Play? Junior-age nonfiction as objects of design.' In *Reading: literacy and language.* Vol 35: 3, 106-110

Moss, Gemma & Attar, Dena (1999) 'Boys and Literacy: Gendering the reading curriculum.' In Prosser, J. *School Culture.* London: Paul Chapman.

O'Neill, Amanda (1995) *I wonder why: Spiders spin webs.* London: Kingfisher

Royston, Angela (1992) *Eye-openers: Minibeasts.* London: Dorling Kindersley

CHAPTER 10

Starting with enthusiasm:

Linking ICT and Literacy

Sue McGonigle

A group of Year 5 boys' enthusiasm in the computer suite contrasted markedly with their lack of enthusiasm for writing in the classroom. This provided the catalyst for enabling them to create purposeful texts using ICT.

Raising boys' achievement has been an issue for us at Lee Manor School for several years. As non-class based Deputy Head I have been able to follow this through by attending courses and conferences on this theme. I have taken the issues and points raised back into school, discussed them with colleagues and planned action in school. As an example of this we had a school focus on male role models, and held a highly successful 'Dads in school day'. We planned this carefully to include an event that fathers (and other male relatives/carers) could participate in. This included a riotous 'countdown' quiz as well as the opportunity to meet and talk to teachers about literacy teaching. The day was written up in the local paper and formed the focus for a display of photos and then a school book. It led to regular visits and greater involvement by this group of dads.

This initiative, and most of our previous work on boys' achievement, has focused predominantly on reading, with improving motivation a key factor. We wanted now to expand this to writing and were aware of the gaps between boys' and girl's achievement in writing. This led me to come on the Boys and Writing project. From the areas covered and from discussions with colleagues on the project and school I decided that motivation in writing was an obvious area for development. I was particularly interested in Gemma Moss's research that identified the 'can and don't' group of boys in reading. I knew there was a group of boys who can and don't write in our school and wanted to follow this up.

I was interested in investigating how far creating real purposes for writing had a positive impact on motivation. Writing for an audience is something we have tried to maintain as a school by, for example, encouraging children to write

> I was interested in investigating how far creating real purposes for writing had a positive impact on motivation.

to authors or make books for younger children. Last year we took this a step further when we became linked with a school in Ghana and two classes exchanged letters with classes in that school. Although I had always felt a sense of purpose and audience was important, I had not investigated how closely this linked to motivation. As a non-class-based deputy I used this project as an opportunity to work closely with a small group of boys and explore this issue.

Baseline information

In discussion with a Year 5 teacher, I discovered she was concerned about three boys who she felt had the ability to write well but lacked interest. I began to gather baseline information on them by looking at their teacher assessments, collecting samples of work, observing lessons and by interviewing them.

Their teacher assessments for writing at the beginning of the year were NC level 3c. When I sampled their work in September it was apparent that it was sometimes unfinished, and there was frequently a lack of understanding of task or purpose. They were not able to sustain writing in different genres. On the CLPE writing scale 2 they would be classified as inexperienced writers.

I observed them during a writing session in class. Although well behaved, they did not contribute to the whole class discussion. When I spoke to them about their work they did not have a clear understanding of the task. I tried to interview them to find out how they felt about writing. They were very reluctant to discuss this with me and so I devised a questionnaire. I felt their most interesting response was to the question:

'Who are you writing for at school?' Their answers were:

'My teacher to see how good you are.'
'For the teachers to stick on the wall.'
'Poems and information are for the teacher but sometimes messages are for other people.'

In the classroom I noted they did enjoy working with a partner on the speaking and listening activity. However, I observed that all three avoided being the scribe.

The second occasion I went to work with them, they were in the computer suite and I was struck by the contrast to the previous occasion. They listened carefully to instructions. They were animated and enthusiastic, working collaboratively, discussing ideas and suggesting improvements. All three of them were at ease and very focused.

Using ICT

We had on the 'Boys and Writing' course spent a session exploring and discussing the potential of ICT in literacy and particularly the interest that boys show in using ICT at home and school. We had looked particularly at the potential for using ICT in writing. This promised to be a profitable area to follow up and I decided to base my project on devising ways to create a sense of purpose and audience by using ICT in writing. I also wanted to exploit the exciting

The second occasion I went to work with them, they were in the computer suite and I was struck by the contrast to the previous occasion.

potential offered by our new computer suite.

I aimed to see if using the computers would help to make clear the purpose and audience for writing and would improve this group of boys' motivation to write. I had a relatively limited amount of time to work with the group so planned two activities which I thought would provide opportunities to exploit some different aspects of using ICT for literacy, one involving e-mailing and publication via a web site and the other a longer project using Hyper-studio.

Publishing on the Web

The idea for the first activity came after our local book supplier contacted us to request work from pupils to post on their new web site. I decided this would be a very easy way to show the boys that writing could be for a purpose and have, in this case, a very wide audience. I arranged a visit to the bookshop where they were able to meet the web site designer and watch him working. They met the manager and he let them browse and choose books to take away. He asked them if they would review one of them for the web site.

On our return to school we did this as a shared writing activity so that the boys would not find the writing task onerous and so that they could see the results quickly. We e-mailed the review to the book company and within a few days the boys were able to see their work on the web, show their class in the computer suite and share it with the rest of the school in assembly. This gave the group considerable satisfaction and pride in their achievement, and provided the impetus for other children to follow suit. Now other children have work posted on this website and one boy, relatively disaffected as a rule, was so inspired that he wrote a review at home and has had his work published on the website too.

I decided to follow the success of this activity with a longer task. I wanted to involve the boys in collaborative writing based on their own interests that used computers and had a very clear purpose and audience, which the boys themselves would decide. We had just received Inset as a staff on Hyper-studio and this package seemed to be an obvious choice. I was very fortunate to be able to work closely with Jill Hunt, the classroom assistant who had taken on the new role of offering ICT support. Jill showed the boys the types of interactive projects that could be done using Hyper-studio and then I talked to them about what they would like to make and who it would be for.

An interactive story

Inspired partly by the books they had just reviewed and also by their own interests they chose to write an interactive football story. Their stated audience was: 'Anyone who likes football'. Some of the writing was composed on

paper and some on screen. A range of writing was involved including, planning, narrative, interview, labels. They also had to record their voices, so the project included a performance element. They were working collaboratively throughout and whether they were working with me on paper or with Jill in the computer suite we found the best approach was to try to create a situation where the boys were working independently but had adult guidance when they needed it. They went on to share their work with other children and could see the reaction of their chosen audience.

The motivation of the boys was very apparent throughout this project. They were keen to give up lunch times or PE if necessary to finish it. That looked as if it might be necessary when all their work was wiped off at one point!

When I talked to them about it they said they enjoyed working together and liked using their interests as a starting point. They enjoyed learning how to animate their story and said that it was fun to record their voices. They especially like the varied approach in their football story with lots for the reader to do. They were quite happy to do the writing involved and saw it as one of the processes that led to their end product. They are very proud of the result.

Evaluation

It was clear that linking writing and ICT had been a successful and enjoyable writing experience for these boys. Motivation for these activities had been high.

I was also interested in whether this project had had any impact on their class work. Their class teachers reported that they had noticed a marked improvement in motivation in one of the boys in particular. He is now much more likely to participate in whole class discussions, he is able to sustain interest in writing tasks for longer periods of time and has a clearer

> They were quite happy to do the writing involved and saw it as one of the processes that led to their end product. They are very proud of the result.

understanding of task and purpose.

When I presented these findings to the Boys and Writing Conference I summarised what I considered to be the key aspect of this project under the following headings:

- The boys were highly motivated during this project.
- They were very clear about the purpose and audience.
- They enjoyed working collaboratively.
- They liked using their own interests.
- They were pleased with the variety in the finished product with lots for the reader to do.
- They enjoyed using computers, and in particular animating their story and recording their voices.
- They saw the writing involved as one of the processes that led to their end product rather than an end in itself.

I have shared these findings with colleagues in school and they provided a useful checklist for using to reflect on boys' attitude to writing tasks.

I am trying to find more ways of developing this sense of audience and purpose using ICT. My Year 6 'booster group' prepared a report on the school for our forthcoming website. The website, when it is up and running will provide a wonderful way for the children to publish their work. We plan to use e-mail more widely, perhaps even one day to communicate with our partner school in Ghana!

Sue McGonigle
Lee Manor Primary School,
London Borough of Lewisham

References

Moss, Gemma (1998) *The Fact and Fiction Research Project. Interim Findings* Southampton, University of Southampton Centre for Language in Education

CHAPTER 11

Tuning into boys' interest in the early years

Sue Hirschheimer

Already in the nursery school, some boys avoid quiet literacy activities. In the nursery described here some writing deliberately linked to physical activities. Sending messages has also involved boys in writing – but too early an emphasis on correctness can trigger resistance.

I was interested in how to encourage boys in a nursery school setting to choose to make marks, in order to lay firm foundations for them to become confident writers. Experience has shown that many boys in the early years tend to choose action-based activities and may show reluctance to join in quieter, structured tasks. Many of our boys in the year when the Boys and Writing project took place were keenly motivated to run, climb, ride bikes and play with cars and trains alongside their peers. I looked at a range of strategies that might involve these boys in writing and in this article I focus on two of these.

While many girls will come readily to join adults at an activity sitting at a table, an invitation to some boys to join the same activity can produce a number of avoidance tactics. Ignoring the invitation, pretending they did not hear, or connecting briefly with the activity just to please the adult are some of the ways that boys tend to respond. Left to themselves, many boys seem to choose activities that involve action and space.

The main focus of my research has considered two main strategies and how boys have responded quite positively in choosing to be involved.

Encouraging active mark-making

This strategy has involved having really large pieces of paper available for children to use as they wish, but ensuring that adults are there to support their activity. Boys particularly have responded to being with their peers and their friends, engaged in active mark-making, using whole body actions and making use of all the space available.

John and Carl, two boys who enjoy being active, came to the block area together. A large roll of

> While many girls will come readily to join adults at an activity sitting at a table, an invitation to some boys to join the same activity can produce a number of avoidance tactics

paper and a pot of felt pens were available. They explored the space, moving the pens up and down, walking, crawling along to the end of the paper. In this way, they drew several long lines up and down, getting faster and faster. They turned this into a racing game, making their pens race and laughing with each other. One of them started making dabbing marks and so did the other. They made quite high jabbing movements with their arms. Then they started jumping up and down copying each other and seeming to take turns.

John started rolling with his whole body along the paper, Carl copied him chanting "Roll over Roll over" in a sing song voice (from the song Ten in the Bed). I said to them "You're going over and over, and round and round." John made his pen make large circular movements. They took the cylinder blocks off the shelf. John rolled them about at first but then started building them up. The session finished when the blocks fell down a couple of times after the boys had built them up. They both left the area together.

The children's physical movements seemed to be linked to their marks on the paper. The jumping up and down came after they had made jabbing movements on the paper. The circular marks were made after they had rolled over and over. Do children need to make these representative marks, and do the marks relate to the movements of their bodies, as when they climb and ride bikes? Does their learning of body control have a physical and cognitive link to their learning to use pens to make marks?

Using large sheets and rolls of paper have now become an integral part of our practice. The rolls are available and, while they are not necessarily put out each day, staff and children can access them readily.

Message pots

Our use of message pots derives from the Italian early years schools in Reggio Emilia, where the 'Hundred Languages of Children' are celebrated. These schools use communication boxes to encourage children to communicate with each other in a real and meaningful way. The boxes are in a central place in the school and are like pigeon-holes, designed to take notes, cards, and objects.

We decided to institute 'message pots'. The pot idea was built on our use of storage pots for the children's pictures. We made the pots out of

transparent mineral water bottles, with the children's photos and names on them. All the staff also have their own message pots. We found many uses for the message pots. Children sent Christmas cards to their friends and

> Some boys have become particularly interested in their message pots. They have really responded to receiving messages and have wanted to respond to them.

parents helped them to 'post' the cards in the message pots, matching names to photos. Staff sent cards at Christmas and also send individual messages to children. Many children have started sending their own messages to each other; they regularly send party invitations via the message pots. Some boys have become particularly interested in their message pots. They have really responded to receiving messages and have wanted to respond to them.

Mark found an envelope in his message pot. He became very excited about this and went around holding it in his hand. Eventually he was persuaded to open it and an adult helped him read it. It was a Christmas card from Hayley. Mark was very excited and had to go all over the nursery to find Hayley. "Did you give me a birthday card?" (An adult helped him remember it was a Christmas card). Holly said "Yes." Mark said "Thanks!" Hayley said "You're welcome!" Mark said "I'm going to make you one." Mark went off and with the help of an adult made a card with a Christmas stamp. He asked me to write first and said "Then I'll do a bit." He wrote M for Mark and made some xxxx for kisses. He posted it in Hayley's message pot.

Jim's Birthday

Jim the guinea pig had his own message pot and children were keen to make birthday cards and messages when we celebrated his birthday. Many children posted cards and messages in his pot. Several of the boys are very interested in Jim, they love stroking him when he comes out of his run, and love to bring him carrots and apples. This interest was developed and children were encouraged to make a big, shared card for Jim. Many of the boys joined in this activity and enjoyed "writing" together. Much of their mark-making consisted of large circular or up and down movements and not necessarily of letter-like shapes going from left to right.

It seemed important to accept what the children could do and to welcome the fact that they had had the confidence to make marks together. Any attempt to focus on the formal conventions of writing at this stage might well have put the children off. Our experience with young children has shown us that an insistence on adult expectations of the "right" way to do things – especially when it comes to writing - can result in avoidance tactics. Many times we have heard young children saying "I can't" when specific outcomes are expected in writing. This is why it seems more important for children to try, to have a go, and to get involved, even though many are not yet ready to produce "conventional writing" at three and four years old.

Other Strategies

While these strategies have involved a number of boys in mark-making, there are other tactics, that have helped us to think how to involve boys and all children in choosing to write and be interested in writing and mark-making.

• Promoting self esteem and confidence

As well as verbal acknowledgement of children's achievements, the use of photographs and video to document their achievements helps to reinforce their positive behaviour and to share it with their peers and families. Documenting what children do provides them with very good models of how we can record experience and look back on it with the help of images and writing.

• Working with families

It helps when adults are genuinely interested in and give time to what children are interested in. Adults need to value children's early marks, focusing on what they can do rather than what they cannot do. This often means working closely with families and encouraging them to recognise children's early achievements. Experience has shown that parents tend to value the correct formation of letters and take little notice of other signs of progress.

• Modelling writing and shared writing

As adults in the nursery we spend time modelling writing in a variety of contexts: writing for ourselves - notes, observations, messages, on the computer; writing for the children - scribing their stories, writing notes about their models and paintings, and so on.

• An inviting writing area and adequate resources

Writing areas need to offer children a range of possibilities for writing and mark-making in different formats. But just as importantly, writing resources need to be available in or nearby all the main areas of the nursery; the role play area, the blocks and construction area, the small world play area, the technology, painting and computer areas, and particularly outside. Having large pieces of paper and a range of pens available both indoors and outdoors has motivated many children, and particularly boys, to move between their activities and drawing or writing.

• Writing for meaning.

Finding real, purposeful ways of engaging children in making marks is one of the keys to supporting boys' writing development. We have found that most children respond to the opportunity to communicate with others in writing. We have a constant flow of letters, messages, birthday cards, festival cards (Eid, Divali, Christmas, Easter etc) going round the nursery. Celebrating Jim the guinea pig's birthday motivated many children.

> Finding real, purposeful ways of engaging children in making marks is one of the keys to supporting boys' writing development.

Superhero play and play based on TV fictions

Most children draw much of their play from TV and videos that they have seen. Adults need to acknowledge these interests and join in with children's themes. But they can also channel repetitive play in a more positive way - making suggestions, bringing in other characters, adding writing resources.

If writing is viewed as a natural part of all these activities, just as it is part of our daily activities outside school, children can come to see writing and mark-making as normal and enjoyable, rather than as a formal and sometimes intimidating activity where the focus is on correctness.

Sue Hirschheimer
Tunstall Nursery School,
London Borough of Croydon

CHAPTER 12

Multimodal narratives

Eve Bearne

Taking off from a study of the content and media influences in children's writing, Eve Bearne compares written and pictorial texts in boys' and girls' stories, and finds boys making more use of images in structuring narratives. As they draw on multimedia sources, what problems are boys likely to meet in constructing written texts?

Texts and stereotypes

Zoe got me a present. She got me a Manchester United football kit. The new one that is.. Mike got p****d off really bad because I'm going out with Zoe and he really really loves her but she don't love him not one little bit.

This extract from a football romance story by a Year 5 boy confounds some assumptions made about boys' writing. As part of an analysis about gender and writing, Peter Thomas, chief examiner for one of the GCSE boards, argues that boys do less well in examinations because they are 'less subtle and skilful than girls of an equivalent age'. He uses driving as a metaphor:

If anything shows the differences between men and women it is their attitude to cars and driving. Women tend to want safe and comfortable transport. Men like power, instruments and technical options… Boys' stories often have pace and event at the expense of anything else. As narrative drivers, they see the road ahead as their own, an invitation to celebrate solo potency, to put themselves or their character in the driving seat. It's the ability to respond to a passenger, and to the landscape, as well as to have a purpose for the journey, which makes for good travelling.
(Thomas 1997)

It just won't do to fall into easy stereotypes like this about boys' and girls' writing, although it would be fair to point out that this was written five years ago. At about the same time, an Ofsted report summarising recent research on gender and attainment pointed out that, 'Blanket statements about girls performing better than boys or vice versa are difficult to justify' (Arnot et al, 1998). The report emphasises the importance of careful analysis of data, alongside observation of what pupils do. This is equally valid today. There is now strong evidence of boys subverting stereotypical text

> It isn't always a straightforward matter of boys writing stories containing action and /or violence and girls choosing to write about emotions and relationships.

types to reveal a far greater interest in personal relationships and emotions than is more widely acknowledged or noticed. At the same time, whilst there are differences in the ways boys and girls choose to write, what might appear as differences in performance, interest or approach by boys and girls may only be related to surface features. It isn't always a straightforward matter of boys writing stories containing action and /or violence and girls choosing to write about emotions and relationships. The differences are more related to the texts children use as models for writing and this certainly does seem to affect boys' attainment in public examinations. In this chapter I want to look beyond the generalisations to suggest a more differentiated view of what boys and girls are doing as they compose texts.

Action and relationships in young children's texts

I use the word 'text' as well as 'writing' for two reasons. First, because of the shifts taking place in what children read. The increasing availability of multimodal and multimedia texts means that young writers now often draw on highly visual material for their sources and inspiration. Second, because differences in interests and choices which might be associated with gender are apparent long before children have the stamina to represent what they want to say in writing. Asked about the stories they liked, Nursery/Reception and Year 1 classes in a Norfolk infants school mentioned films, television and books:

Boys		Girls	
Thomas the Tank	6	Barbie	6
Power Rangers	6	Fairy tales	6
Teletubbies	4	Teletubbies	6
Hercules	3	Teddy bear stories	3
Toy Story	2	Humpty Dumpty	2
Jurassic Park	2	Pocahontas	1
Action Man	1	Rabbit stories	1
Batman	1	Gerbil stories	1
101 Dalmations	1	Sssh!	1
Tom and Jerry	1	Rosie and Jim	1
Tots TV	1	Tots TV	1
Winnie the Pooh	1	Winnie the Pooh	1

The table shows that with two or three areas of crossover there is a clear pattern of boys choosing action-oriented story types, most of them television or film narratives. The girls, on the other hand, tended to choose stories which reflect relationships between characters and to refer to books and comics/magazines more than boys. In talking about their preferences for books, the boys generally mentioned non-fiction and the girls chose stories about families (Gorman 1998).

When they were asked to draw and tell their own stories, their preferences became equally clear. The children were given large sheets of paper folded to make storyboards. The examples here are representative of the kinds of stories told by all the class. Cemil and Aran (Figs 1 and 2) chose to tell Power Rangers stories. They drew then told the 'story' which their teacher noted for them. Cemil explains his story (Fig.1) :

The Power Rangers make him angry. Ivanoos gets angry with them two. Then one of the Power Rangers fights Ivanoos' dog. And then he fights against him. And then he fights against the three bad people.

Aran (Fig. 2) has the same cast of characters:

They are the Power Rangers and they are fighting Ivanoos' children who are made out of purple stuff. The white one is fighting Ivanoos and the black one is fighting too. They all win and skate away.

In contrast, Jake decides to draw a dinosaur story (Fig. 3):

A long neck dinosaur is eating a tree. Is crying. Tyrannosaurus Rex eating meat. A dinosaur lifting a tree. A Tyrannosaurus Rex looking around. Tyrannosaurus eating. Tyrannosaurus Rex getting sick.

The girls chose more domestic settings for their stories (Figs 4, 5 and 6). Rachael called her story 'A Bear Hunt' (Fig.4):

Us all go to bed. We pretend a monster comes. My mum goes and gets him. My little baby called Charlotte. A big triangle lights up and we look at it. Then my mum wakes up and we wake up too. My baby wakes up. That's my dad.

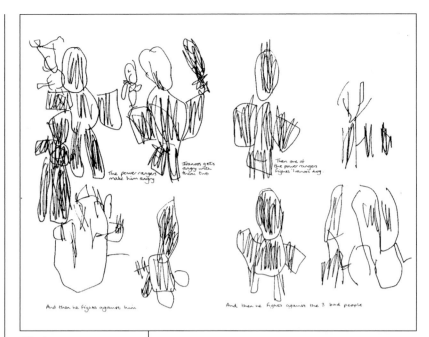

Fig 1

Fig 2

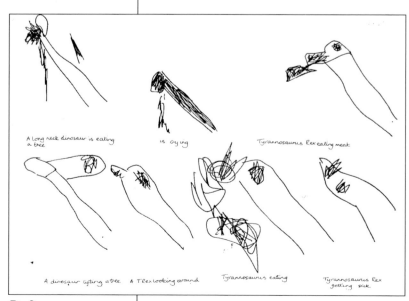

Fig 3

68

Fig 4

Fig 5

Fig 6

Kelly's story (Fig 5) begins by naming the characters:

Me, Mummy, Shane and Daddy. We got out because of the fire. The house was on fire. There was only 8 bricks left then only four bricks left.

Tanith's story was called 'The Snakey':

Once there was a time there were 2 boys. They went out to collect some little eggs and they ran away when they saw an Eastern Ribbon snake from Asia. And the boys rushed in and crashed into one house and told Mummy and Daddy. Then the police took it away and put it in a jar. Then the police took it to the police station. The police took it out of the cage and he got bitten. The police took it to a snake person.

Most of these lack the structure of stories because they have been composed visually first and then described, so that the 'narrative' seems more like captioning in places. Nevertheless, they provide a varied and complex view of the choices made by very young children as they shape their ideas. Taken on face value, the boys (and many of the other boys in the class) have chosen topics which are often associated with boys – action stories and dinosaurs – whilst the girls, again in line with common assumptions, have decided to tell about their homes and families. However, the boys' stories aren't just about action or violence; Cemil picks up the theme of good and evil and Jake 'domesticates' his dinosaurs by describing them crying and getting sick. Similarly, the girls don't just content themselves with domestic narratives: Rachael includes a supernatural event during the night, a courageous mum and dad as a kind of appendix; Kelly describes a fire, carefully enumerating the remaining bricks, and Tanith gives detailed information about the Eastern Ribbon snake. In terms of content, although the boys and girls have chosen apparently expected and perhaps stereotypical settings and characters, the themes and events of their narratives cut across the boundaries of stereotypes.

Pictorial text

Their pictorial text deserves attention, too. Although it is not possible to show this here, the three boys (and many others in the class) chose relatively muted colours – purple, grey, black, brown, whereas the girls used brighter, often primary, colours. Picturebook makers are specific in their choice of colours to create particular effects. Bolder colours are often associated with the imagination, pleasure or jokiness and more sombre colours with monotony, fear, sadness or a bleak emotional landscape. Deciding on colour is just one of the choices made in putting a text together. Cemil and Aran certainly chose colours that they mentioned in their texts and Jake used the camouflage colours specific to his subject matter. With perhaps greater free choice, since their subject matter did not need particular colours, the girls chose to create up-beat, vibrant images.

There are striking differences in the line and shading of the boys' and girls' texts. The girls' strongly outlined front-facing figures contrasting strongly with the more distanced, sketchy figures of the boys' narratives. The most clearly defined full size images coincide with first person narratives as told by Rachael and Kelly. All the children's storyboards showed these differences between boys' and girls' perspective and line. It would be easy to suggest that the boys are simply less assured with their manipulation of their pencils and to invoke ideas of 'fine motor skills'. Attention to the content of the pictures, however, shows careful detail: Aran's Power Rangers put on roller skates and the tiny dots of the rollers certainly don't suggest a lack of coordination and whilst Cemil's colouring shows bravado and verve, it is no less 'inside the lines' than Tanith's or Kelly's. For Kelly and Rachael, individual characters seem to dominate, fitting with the first person narratives, whilst Tanith's and the boys' stories include groups of characters, told about in the third person. A more significant difference, however, lies in the narrative structure of these multimodal texts. Although the narrative structure was governed to a certain extent by the task, there are differences in the ways the boys and girls put their stories together.

In general, the girls tended to tell stories which had more verbal narrative cohesive devices than the boys, although it is arguable whether these genuinely give coherence to Rachael's narrative, for example. In the boys' stories, only Cemil uses conjunctions; in the girls' stories, even Kelly's very brief spoken narrative includes a causal connective and the other two link their narratives with *and* and *then*. Pictorially, in the Power Rangers stories, the boys create cohesion by consistent use of colour for particular characters and by repeating the images of the groups depicted; Jake maintains the angle of each dinosaur's neck as a recurring motif. The girls, however, use colour randomly, even when they are repeating characters. Rachael's mum figure wears different shape and colour clothes, Kelly has no repeat characters although the house changes colour and Tanith only uses colour episodically. It seems, then, that the boys are using pictorial rather than verbal cohesive devices and the girls tend to use verbal rather than image cohesion. At this stage in the writers' development, using connectives and conjunctions does not necessarily tend towards clear narrative structure. It seems that there is greater narrative coherence when the children draw on known narrative patterns, as in the quest-like structures of Cemil's and Aran's Power Rangers stories. The dimensions of structure, choice of setting, character, event and theme in very young boys' and girls'

The theme of the visual text in this book is weaponry. It begins with a centrally placed large handgun on the cover and features a weapon in almost every picture.

1 This was a Year 5/6 class at St Philip's primary school, Cambridge.

multimodal narratives suggest that whilst there may be general preferences for particular subjects for the stories, they are by no means narrowly aligned to concepts of boys-and-action or girls-and-emotions. The differences are more subtly shaped.

Being and doing

Surveys of older children's reading choices often show comparable differences between boys' and girls' preferences to those indicated by younger readers and viewers (Hall and Coles, 2002; Millard, 1997). Whilst there is no doubt that reading and viewing influence writing choices, it would be a mistake to assume that simply because boys prefer action-oriented, quest or adventure stories they are likely to restrict their narratives to action alone. Similarly, it would be misleading to think that girls' preferences for domestic settings and their interest in character signal a lack of action. It isn't just a matter of 'doing' and 'being', although these categories may be useful. In a Cambridge school, during the autumn term, a Year 5/6 class spent part of their literacy time writing a story book[1]. Each book was written with a particular reader in mind. The boys' narratives were largely adventures based on films they were familiar with, for example, *Aliens, Independence Day*, James Bond stories. Several wrote stories where the central characters had to escape from islands; most included monsters, extra-terrestrial beings, aeroplanes, and many included weapons. The chosen readers were mostly male. The girls' narratives tended to draw on their book reading; Jacqueline Wilson, Enid Blyton and Dick King-Smith were particularly influential models for the types of stories chosen. Only two girls drew inspiration from films – *Jumanji* and *Tomb Raider*. Their chosen readers included some males but these were often brothers or friends' younger brothers. From their choice of subjects, it looked as though the class were conforming to type. A closer examination of the books themselves, however, shows as much diversity as in the younger children's narratives.

Arron's novel was titled *Mission Impossible 0902600 Special Edition*. Arron was meticulous about detail both in his drawing and in the language he chose to express his ideas. He did not make many changes between the first draft and the final version (except for spelling and punctuation) but the features he chose to change showed awareness of the role of visual as well as verbal text in telling a story. The cover of his novel shows the influence of video box covers as well as books – the PG sticker, for example. On the final version he has also added 'Free! QUIZ' and a bullet, echoing the covers of magazines. Throughout the text he repeats a little striped logo as a cohesive device. Arron redrafted all his illustrations to include more detail in the final version. In many cases he

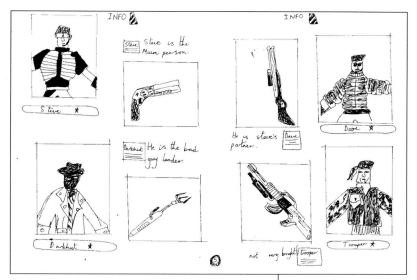

Fig 7

moved from close-up to distance images in order to include more pictorial information. Two pages give details of the main characters and their preferred weapons(Fig 7). In the final version Arron decided to leave out the verbal descriptions of the weapons in every case, although he keeps the background information about the characters. The images of the characters themselves draw on established visual features. The two main characters are in padded combat gear and helmets and their outlines are clear, whereas Darkhut has a cloth mask entirely covering his face and the kind of raincoat seen in American films. Trooper, described by Arron as 'not very bright', is dressed in bandana and camouflage gear – an image drawn from popular culture, magazines and television.

The theme of the visual text in this book is weaponry. It begins with a centrally placed large handgun on the cover and features a weapon in almost every picture (notable because Arron is reflective and shows emotional sensitivity in his relationships). The theme of the verbal text is of comradeship and the conflict between 'good' and 'evil'. Arron adopts an explicit structure, heading his sections: Introduction, The Plot, Info, The Escape, The New Mission, The Ending. The very direct narrative involves the reader immediately: *Let's talk about the case…* suggesting that although some features reflect Arron's reading, he also draws on the kinds of film and television narrative he likes to watch where a voice-over often introduces the action. The visual text follows the structure of action and event and matches the section headings: the first picture is a long shot, setting the scene, the second a picture of one of the main characters mid-shot as he shoots his attacker, the next set are close-ups (half body) of the main characters and mid-shot detailed pictures of their weapons. As the story unfolds, the illustrations move into long shot again featuring the central character. With the increasing close-ups the reader is brought progressively into the text before gradually being moved to a distance again.

There seems no doubt that Arron has deliberately used a variety of visual features to structure the narrative. The verbal text provides the action and emotional content. In contrast to the shooting and interest in weaponry, Steve cries when he sees his friend's body:

He ran out with the plans. He jumped in his car and drove off. He stopped in the middle of the field and saw a dead person looked down and cried. It was Dave. He turned around and got back in his car and went back to his base.

The accompanying illustration shows Steve driving away. The cohesion of Arron's narrative depends on the interrelationship between the visual and verbal text – the use of a repeated motif, the movement between close up and distant perspective, the information carried by the pictorial text so as not to overload the verbal narrative. Arron offers a detailed narrative, set within a death-and-destruction frame drawn from his film and video experience, but with a strong sense of personal relationships and loss. It is a well-designed multimodal text.

Samantha's novel, *A Healthy Farm*, tells a complex story with a great deal of verbal background details about a girl whose one interest is in riding horses. She introduces it like this:

This is a story called A Healthy Farm. *I'll start with Lucy. She goes to a school in Manchester called Romsey. Lucy and her mum live on a farm (so Lucy and her mum look after all the animals). Lucy's dad divorced her mum, well, we won't go into that. I hope you will enjoy the story.*

There is only one illustration within the body of the narrative then a series of pictures included at the end. The one integrated with the story shows a horse and rider – Black Beauty and Lucy. (Fig. 8) The horse is centrally placed, and both are seen side view. The background is of

Fig 8

fluffy clouds and birds against a blue sky. The horse's tail is tightly braided and long. This is a static picture which doesn't relate directly to the narrative but simply shows us the two central 'characters' in an idealised setting. Like Arron, Samantha gives us portraits of the characters – in her case equine and human – involved in the story, but, apart from the cover which introduces Lucy and her mother, all but one are added at the end. All follow the same format: a centrally placed character with no movement, caught as in photographs. Lucy and her mother appear first with Lucy holding up the cup she has won for cross country riding and her mother holding up the cheque for £1,000. They have stylised large smiles and Lucy is wearing her riding helmet and jodhpurs (Fig. 9). The picture summarises the resolution of the

Fig 9

story – success from cross country riding (written on the cup) and a money prize. The similarly stylised blue sky, clouds and birds emphasise the idyllic happiness of the scene. There follow a series of portraits of the characters – Lucy, Lucy's Mum, Black Beauty, Fly Away and Morcely - the three horses mentioned in the story. Where the narrative is packed with detail, dialogue, action, events and adventure (perhaps too many for one novel), the pictorial text is still and stylised. In the written text, Samantha typically uses action verbs; after Black Beauty has been lost, Lucy and her mother search for her for a week then go on holiday where they find a magic carpet which takes them to find Black Beauty:

The carpet wizzed round until at last they saw Black Beauty laying down, they jumped off to see if she was OK. She was fine. Lucy hugged her, "How I've missed you". Beauty nuzzled as if to say I missed you too. Then they went home, Lucy washed her, brushed her coat and made her look lovely again.

The action of the narrative contrasts with the inaction of the images. Clearly Samantha is

Writing from the point of view of 'I' means that the writer has greater control over setting, characters and plot; a personal narrative can only include what the teller is experiencing here and now.

drawing on the kinds of books she has read as well as her personal love for horses. It is noticeable that the narrative movement is carried entirely by the words, as in many of the stories she has read. In comparing Arron's and Samantha's novels, parallels and differences emerge. Both are about competitiveness – winning, defeating others – although Samantha stays mostly within a recognisable, 'domestic' setting and Arron chooses to set his story in the fantasy world of James Bond-type films. Both parade a set of characters but focus on two particularly who share a common cause. Both deal with determination, loyalty and loss. The main differences lie in the multimodal structure of the texts. Arron has designed his narrative to give much of the detail in the pictorial text, using image throughout as a cohesive device. Samantha, on the other hand, structures her narrative almost entirely through the verbal text, using image to summarise, rather than contribute to, the narrative. Each includes emotion and action; just as with the younger children's stories, there is no clear gender distinction here between being and doing. The most important similarity – and difference – lies in the way that each author draws on familiar and preferred texts to shape their own.

Structuring writing

It could be argued that Arron has pulled off a more sophisticated job with his novel. However, when it comes to public assessments of writing (not of *texts*) Samantha's approach is more likely to fit with the requirements. In terms of what counts as valid for purposes other than personal expression – examinations and assessments in general – texts are expected to be written rather than designed. Whilst some young writers find it relatively easy to slip into representing sound, image and movement in words, others end up writing only the words of what in their heads is, in fact, a multimodal text. They are asked for the words, so they supply the words but it is clear that the pictorial and moving elements of their inner narratives are not being represented on the page. As a result their writing is seen as lacking organisation and cohesion, whilst it is very possibly only a partial representation of the full story carried in the mind's eye and ear.

Kunal's story (Fig 10) shows a writer who has a wealth of pictorial images in his head: from the opening filmic setting (we can almost hear the haunting music of a spaghetti western) to the completely unexplained flashback to a previous escapade *Once they tried to murder the President but they got caught* to the comic book image *Spike blew a bubble but it burst and went all over his face*. This may read as a disorganised piece, and the content certainly deserves discussion in terms of gender equity. However, it is clearly based on films he enjoys watching and seen as the synopsis of a feature length film,

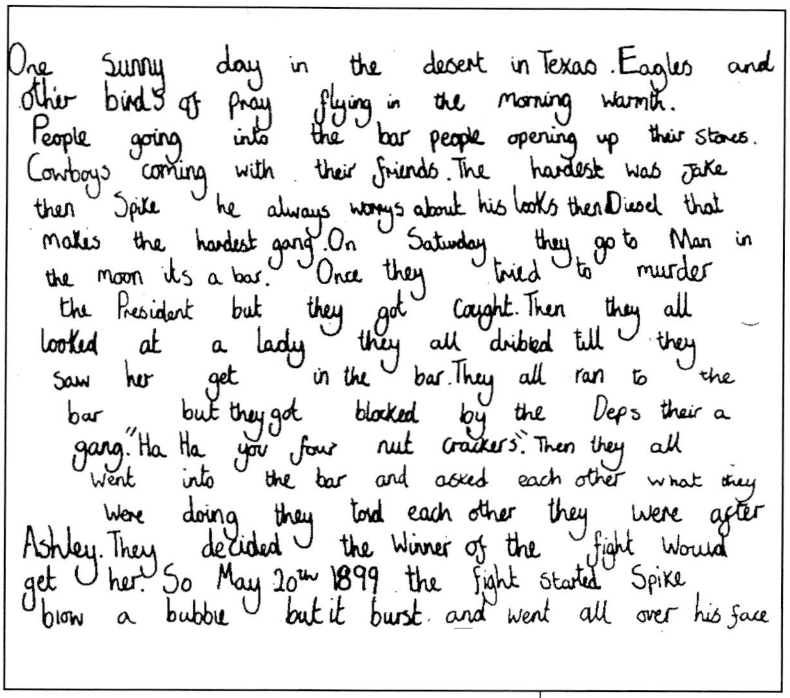

One sunny day in the desert in Texas. Eagles and other birds of pray flying in the morning warmth. People going into the bar people opening up their stores. Cowboys coming with their friends. The hardest was Jake then Spike he always worrys about his looks then Diesel that makes the hardest gang. On Saturday they go to Man in the moon its a bar. Once they tried to murder the President but they got caught. Then they all looked at a lady they all dribled till they saw her get in the bar. They all ran to the bar but they got blocked by the Deps their a gang. "Ha Ha you four nut crackers". Then they all went into the bar and asked each other what they were doing they told each other they were after Ashley. They decided the winner of the fight would get her. So May 20th 1899 the fight started Spike blow a bubble but it burst and went all over his face

Fig 10

accompanied by snatches of footage, it begins to read much more like a summary or even a trailer. Kunal is quite competent technically. He would benefit from discussion of the different ways in which written and visual texts are put together and the ways in which they are read.

Different types of text have varying patterns of cohesion which contribute to the overall shape or architecture of the text. Narrative or report depend on chronological cohesion; texts which are represented visually or diagrammatically depend on spatial cohesion. In films, cohesion depends on repeated visual motifs, perspective, close-up on characters' faces or exchanged glances, choices of setting, colour, intensity of light, the organisation of time sequences, the use of musical or sound patterns to underpin the affective elements of the text… as well as the text cohesion of dialogue, the connectives, conjunctions, pronoun references, deixis, substitution, ellipsis, lexical patterns. In picture books, lines, vectors, the direction of characters' eye gaze and spatial organisation act as visual connectives and conjunctions; repeated visual motifs echo the text cohesion in narrative verbal text created by lexical repetition or ties; gesture and stance, sustained and changed through framing, as well as depicted action, give narrative cohesion.

Children now have available to them many forms of text which include sound, voices, intonation, stance, gesture, movement, as well as print and image. These have changed the ways in which young readers expect to read; it has changed the way they think, the ways they construct meaning. It seems that boys draw on their multimodal and multimedia experience more than girls who tend to use written texts as models (see, for example, Graham 2000 and Moss 2000). But trying to capture a visual model

in writing is a far more expansive (and perhaps demanding) task than drawing on certain kinds of written models. Film and video texts are essentially third person narratives; unless they use voiceover, the stories have to be told 'from the outside'. Transforming a visual text into writing requires the depiction of broad vistas, a wide range of characters, several linked events, an emotional landscape evoked by music, colour and perspective. Hardy, a writer who anticipates film in his broadscapes balanced with close-ups, took whole novels to tell his stories. Young writers who use film as inspiration but who have to write for about 45 minutes without much time to redraft, are not likely to be able to capture all that they want to. And how does a writer know how to resolve a narrative if the imaginative impulse comes from computer games whose structure is repetitive and recurrent? It is much harder to transform these sources than to base a story on the first person narratives of, for example, Jacqueline Wilson. Writing from the point of view of 'I' means that the writer has greater control over setting, characters and plot; a personal narrative can only include what the teller is experiencing here and now. Added to this, using books as models means that readers have experience of how sound and visual effects are expressed in words.

I don't want to make this sound too simplistic. Girls also draw on their experience of visual texts and there are, of course, boys who write first person locally set narratives. I am not arguing for young writers being encouraged always to make multimodal narratives rather than continuous prose. There are times when we want to read written texts, times when we choose to read texts which include images and times when we want to watch film, video and television. Young writers need experience of composing in a range of modes and media. However, the texts I have looked at in his chapter suggest that there are important differences in the ways boys and girls tend to construct texts which reflect their reading and viewing choices. Children deserve to be given greater scope in their text-making by explicit discussion of variations in the structures, purposes and effects of multimodal as well as written texts. For this to happen, teachers themselves need to know how such texts work and to be aware of just how sophisticated and complex young children's multimodal narratives can be.

Eva Bearne
University of Cambridge, Faculty of Education

My thanks are due to Jane Brooks, Gayle Gorman and the children in their classes for allowing me to present their work here.

References

Coles, Martin and Hall, Christine (2002) 'Gendered readings: learning from children's reading choices' in *Journal of Research in Reading* Vol 25 Number 1 February 2002 pp 96-108

Gorman, Gayle (1999) unpublished essay *Story and Gender in the Early Years* written as part of the Advanced Diploma in Language, Literature and Literacy, Homerton College, Cambridge

Graham, Lynda 'From Tyrannosaurus to Pokemon: autonomy in the teaching of writing' in *Reading literacy and language* Volume 35 number 1, April 2001 pp 18-26

Millard, Elaine (1997) *Differently Literate: Boys, Girls and the Schooling of Literacy* London, Falmer Press

Moss, Gemma (2000) 'Raising boys' attainment in reading: some principles for intervention' *Reading* Volume 34 Number 3, November 2000 pp 101 – 106

Thomas, Peter (1997) 'Doom to the Red-eyed Nyungghns from the Planet Glarg' *English in Education* Vol 31 No 3